George Bruce Malleson

Captain Musafir's Rambles in Alpine lands

George Bruce Malleson

Captain Musafir's Rambles in Alpine lands

ISBN/EAN: 9783743330368

Manufactured in Europe, USA, Canada, Australia, Japa

Cover: Foto ©ninafisch / pixelio.de

Manufactured and distributed by brebook publishing software (www.brebook.com)

George Bruce Malleson

Captain Musafir's Rambles in Alpine lands

THE KRÄUMEYER'S HOUSE.

CAPTAIN MUSAFIR'S
RAMBLES IN ALPINE LANDS.

BY

COLONEL G. B. MALLESON, C.S.I.

Illustrated by
G. STRANGMAN HANDCOCK.

"I've taught me other tongues, and in strange eyes
Have made me not a stranger."
CHILDE HAROLD.

LONDON:
W. H. ALLEN & CO., 13 WATERLOO PLACE. S.W.

1884.

(All rights reserved.)

Inscribed,

BY PERMISSION,

TO

IN WHOM TWENTY YEARS HAVE NOT DIMINISHED
THE GENIALITY,
NOR CLOUDED OVER THE BRIGHTNESS,
WHICH RENDERED HER THE LIFE OF OUR PARTY
IN 1863.

Christmas Day,
1883.

PREFACE.

AFTER a residence of nearly fifteen years in India, to which country I had proceeded at the early age of seventeen, I paid, in 1858, my first visit to Germany. With the tastes for mountaineering, for exploring, and for fly-fishing which I possessed, I very soon realised the fact that, whilst the southern portions of that country offered a field for enjoyment practically unlimited, yet that enjoyment could only be perfectly realised by those who could speak easily the language of the people.

I did not then possess that accomplishment. So penetrated, however, was I with the charms of Bavaria and Austria, that on my return to India I devoted myself with assiduity to the study of German. Fortune greatly befriended me in my masters. They were both—for during the four years of my study I had two—privates in the 38th Regiment:— and they were both very remarkable men. The first, Henry Blochmann, was the youngest son but one of a book-seller at Dresden. Naturally very clever, his talents had been fully developed at the University of Leipzig. There he had mastered, besides the literature of France and Germany, Latin, Greek, Hebrew, and Arabic. His thorough acquaintance with the last-named language prompted his father to send him to Paris to push his fortunes in connection with Algeria. Circumstances, into which it is not necessary to enter, occurred at Paris which decided Blochmann to throw up all his prospects and embark on a new career. Every young German has one specially intimate friend, his second self, his "du," or "thou." The "du" of Blochmann was a young man, somewhat older than himself, named Jäkel, the son of a merchant at Breslau, and occupying a position in a mercantile house in Silesia. Blochmann wrote to Jäkel a letter, in which, stating that circumstances having rendered it necessary that he should quit France and not return to Germany he had decided to enlist as a private in the English army, he summoned him, in the name of friendship, to join him at Paris, to accompany him to England, and to enlist with him. He added that the prospects in the British army were excellent, as a mutiny was raging in India, and, in all probability, they would both soon become officers.

Without a moment's hesitation Jäkel locked up his desk, resigned his office, and made his way to Paris. He found Blochmann anxiously expecting him. Between them, the two friends could raise a sufficient sum to pay their way to London and defray their expenses for about a week. Although Blochmann was thoroughly grounded in other languages, he did not know a word of English. Jäkel shared his ignorance. The out-look before the two travellers was certainly not promising.

However, they started, arrived in London, and managed to find their way to the Horse-Guards. On the road thither Blochmann stopped at the shop of the publishers of this book, and purchased a grammar of the Hindustani language. Something whispered to him, he has told me, when narrating his story, that his knowledge of Arabic would render the study of Hindustani easy, and that acquaintance with that language could not but help him on in his new career. At the Horse Guards in 1857 the late Sir Henry Storks occupied a prominent position. Sir Henry Storks understood French thoroughly, and to him the two aspirants were introduced. Sir Henry listened to their story, granted their prayer, and sent them to his own regiment, the 38th Foot, then at Colchester, under orders for India.

A few days after the young men had joined the regiment, the capabilities of Blochmann, who had devoted himself with assiduity to his Hindustani Grammar, were recognised. He was excused all duty, and appointed instructor in general to the officers. That position he held not only during the short stay of the regiment at Colchester, but throughout the period of the voyage to India. From first to last he never was in the ranks. So exemplary was his conduct, and so much did he impress his commanding officer by his intelligence and his high qualities, that, on arriving in Calcutta, he was appointed, with the grade of sergeant, to a small post in one of the offices in Fort William. He was holding that post when, in 1859, I made his acquaintance, and arranged with him that he should read with me for an hour daily.

I may add that Blochmann had not been more than six months in India before he passed the examination, called the Higher Standard, in the native languages—an examination which very few officers indeed dare approach under two years, that he then bought his discharge, and, rising from post to post, became ultimately Principal of the Madrasah, and a Gold Medallist and M.A. of the University of Calcutta. His translation of the Ain-i-Akbari, his great attainments as a Persian and Arabic scholar, had secured him a reputation spreading even to the learned in Europe, when he was unhappily cut off by cholera in 1878.

When Blochmann was my instructor he had not become famous. He gave to me, however, the benefit of the qualities which made him famous afterwards, and I must ever feel a debt of gratitude to him for the pains which he took to ground me in the knowledge of his own language. He did not cease his instruction until I had thoroughly mastered all its intricacies and all its difficulties.

I read with Blochmann for more than two years and a half. He ceased his instruction because, by that time, his avocations had become so numerous that he wanted for himself the time which he had, till then, devoted to me. He and I were both anxious too, at this time, that something should be done for his devoted friend, Jäkel.

Jäkel had not had the good fortune of Blochmann. He possessed no knowledge of Eastern languages to save him from drudgery. He had gone, then, into the ranks, had learned his drill, had accompanied the regiment to Audh, and had earned the character of being a sober, steady, trustworthy soldier.

After he had been a year with the regiment, a circumstance happened which reflects alike on the character of Jäkel and the composition of the regiment to which he belonged. The 38th was an Irish regiment. A very large proportion of the privates could neither read nor write. Many of those who could read and write possessed certain disqualifications. Thus it happened that when, at the period of which I am writing, the post of schoolmaster-sergeant fell vacant, the commanding officer selected Jäkel to fill it. No mean testimony, this, to the character and qualifications of the young German who had joined the regiment the year before, absolutely ignorant of the English language!

Jäkel remained schoolmaster-sergeant for about a year.

PREFACE. ix

At a subsequent period he told me that he managed during that time to read every book in the regimental library. When all the books had been finished, his resources were exhausted. The society of his illiterate companions brought him no pleasure. Gradually he pined away. That disease, so common to the German race, Heimweh—yearning for home—mastered him, and he became seriously ill. In his extremity he wrote to Blochmann, imploring him, in his turn, to make a sacrifice to friendship and to buy his discharge.

It was about this time that I first heard of Jäkel. Blochmann had never mentioned his name before; but shortly after Jäkel had made to him the despairing appeal of which I have spoken, he came to me, told me the story as I have told it here, assured me that he had forwarded the money with the application for his friend's discharge, but had received in reply a communication to the effect that the application could not be granted unless an officer of position would sign an engagement that he would give the applicant employment: he concluded by entreating me to sign such an engagement. I then held a high position in the Military Audit Office, in which vacancies were constantly occurring. I, therefore, at once signed the paper.

Jäkel was discharged in due course, and joined my office. I found him quiet, attentive, painstaking and assiduous. But his days of adventure were only beginning. He was returning one day from office to his house, when he came face to face with one of the leading German merchants of Calcutta, beside whom he had sat as a boy on the benches of the High School at Breslau. The recognition was mutual: so likewise was the pleasure. It chanced that that very evening I met the merchant in question dining with the Lieutenant-Governor at Alipúr. He related to me the inci-

b

dent, and begged me to allow him to take care of the fortunes of Jäkel. I, of course, consented, and a few days later Jäkel was transferred on an increased salary from the Audit Department to a merchant's office.

It was shortly after this that Blochmann's avocations compelled him to give up his instruction, and I took Jäkel in his place. With him a different system was adopted. We never looked at grammars or dictionaries; we only conversed. Every morning he gave me a most delightful hour; for he had been a great traveller, had visited every part of Southern Germany and of Italy, and had made the best use of his opportunities. He was, besides, a born conversationist; was large-minded, sympathising, and generous—in a word, a most pleasant companion. He interested me so much, that I made use of what interest I possessed to obtain for him an appointment in the Bengal Police Department, an appointment which would have been a life-provision. The berth was actually obtained, when, just at the moment, the German merchant offered him the charge of one of his tea plantations in Assam. After some hesitation, Jäkel accepted the latter offer, and set out for that province.

About the same time my wife and I made our second visit to Europe to undertake the tour in Southern Germany, the details of which form the main subject of this book. Before I refer to that, I may conclude, as far as I am aware of it, the career of my Silesian friend.

Jäkel went to Assam, and there, as everywhere, conducted himself well. But after he had resided on the tea-garden about a year and a half, a very severe attack of malarious fever forced him to return to Europe. He must have crossed me on my return passage, as he arrived at Trieste just as I reached Calcutta. When he landed at Trieste, Jäkel found that the Archduke Maximilian was raising troops to accompany him to Mexico. The venture was just of the kind to appeal to an enthusiastic nature such as his. He offered himself, produced his credentials, was accepted, and given the rank of lieutenant.

In Mexico Jäkel did not derogate one inch from his high character. He behaved with so much courage and gallantry that before long he was appointed, with the rank of captain, to the Imperial Guard, and was, I have been informed, specially selected to accompany the unfortunate Empress to Europe when the fortunes of her husband were threatened with calamity. Since that time I have not heard of him; but I feel confident that, wherever he may have been, he has always conducted himself as a loyal and true-hearted gentleman.

I began by saying that both my instructors were remarkable men, and I think I have proved the statement. For what they taught me, and for the manner in which they taught it, I never can, I repeat, be sufficiently grateful.

As to the tour which I made immediately after the completion of my four years' studies, I will let the account speak for itself. I will only add that, at the request of many of our friends in India, who contemplated a similar journey, I inserted my journal in the form of an article in the *Calcutta Review*, and that it appears now as it appeared in that excellent periodical, with all its original enthusiasm and, I might perhaps add, with all its audacity.

Since that first introduction into the country which may be called the Paradise of the World, I have made many incursions into Austria. There is scarcely a village in Carniola, in Carinthia, in the two Austrias, and but few in Tirol, in the Bavarian Highlands, and in Styria, which I have not visited; hardly a mountain stream which I have not, however slightly, despoiled.

Seven years after the first glimpses of the promised Land recorded in this volume, we again visited Europe. This time, also, we landed at Trieste, and proceeded at once, by way of Laibach, into Carniola. The charms, the loveliness, of that beautiful province, it would be impossible to exaggerate. Veldes, Feistriz, the Wochein See, the glorious Terglou, and many kindred places hardly less admirable, rise up to give mental evidence in support of this assertion. After a stay at Veldes of more than a fortnight spent in climbing, rambling, and fishing, we proceeded to the scarcely less beautiful Wurzener Thal, the delight of Sir Humphrey Davy, with its Lengenfeld, its Wurzen, its Weissenfels, and its Tarvis. From the second of these places we crossed the Karavankas to Villach and Klagenfurt, and proceeded thence through Styria to our old haunts in the Salzkammergut; thence, after a stay of some time, to the Bavarian Highlands— the pleasure of the exploring of which was greatly increased by the society of some charming Bavarian friends—passing down by the Achensee, visiting Partenkirchen and Garmisch, and winding up with the Passion play at Ober-Ammergau. The year following, the same beautiful country was invaded from the south, by way of Verona, Bozen, and Innsbruck, the valleys and mountains near which were visited, and thence by way of Nüremberg, Carlsbad, and Prague to Berchtesgaden, there to make a prolonged stay. In the neighbourhood of that place we rented, with a friend, the little inn at Unterstein, mentioned in these pages, and made excursions to Ramsau, Reichenhall, the Hintersee, and, subsequently, down to the beautiful Zell-am-see.

On my final return from India, in 1877, I attacked the

country from a new base. Again landing at Trieste, I proceeded with a friend by rail to Görz (Gorizia), and drove thence, by way of Canale to Tolmino, and from Tolmino by way of Podmenz and Coritenza to Podberda, a country abounding in the most magnificent scenery. At Podberda we quitted the einspänner, and crossed on foot the Schwarzenberg, a part of the South-eastern Alps, to Feistritz. The range was not lofty—about six thousand and forty feet,—but the walk was memorable from the curious difference between the temperature on its northern and southern sides. It was the month of May, and we were ascending from the south. Half an hour after we started the rain fell heavily, and continued to fall during nearly the entire period of the climb upwards. On reaching the summit, we found that during the same time snow had fallen heavily on the northern side. The descent, I recollect, was rendered more difficult by the fact that darkness set in before we had reached the plain, and we had to trust to our instinct to guide us. However, we reached the little inn at Feistritz about 9 P.M., and found my old friend the landlord happy to give us a welcome—and a good dinner.

Since that period scarcely a year has passed which has not seen me in one or other of the seven charming provinces—in the two Austrias, or in Tirol, or in Styria, or in Carniola, or in Carinthia, or in the Bavarian Highlands, or in all. The warm-hearted, manly, generous, and kindly people who inhabit them always give me a welcome, and make me feel that they regard me as a friend. It is difficult to say too much in their praise. To an independence of character, assured to them by the fact that the soil they cultivate is their own, they add great modesty, sensibility to kindness, and, in very many instances, an intelligence which would put to the blush the acquirements of men belonging to a station in life far above their own. Of all these journeys I have kept notes, and possibly some of these notes would give information regarding parts of the country far less visited and less known, though not less charming, than those mentioned in these pages. But they would want, I fear, the freshness, the sense of delightful novelty, the feeling of anticipations more than realised, which possessed me on the first occasion. There is, too, another reason why I have selected the original series for publication in preference to any other. That series appeared, I have said, in the pages of the *Calcutta Review*, and I am bound to add that it was very well received. I have often been asked to allow the papers to appear in a collected form, but I have always refused. Very recently, however, my friend, Mr. Strangman Handcock, was kind enough to illustrate some of the places visited by a series of pen-and-ink sketches. The great talent shown in these evoked a desire on my part that they should be submitted to the approbation of a larger circle than I can command; and, in now carrying out this desire, I have only to express an earnest hope that the shortcomings of the writer may be forgotten in the approval which will, I am sure, be bestowed upon the sketcher.

G. B. MALLESON.

27 *West Cromwell Road*,
   South Kensington.

CONTENTS.

	PAGE
PREFACE	v
PART I.—From India to the Salzkammergut	1
PART II.—In Bavaria and Switzerland	57
PART III.—The Salzkammergut, Tirol, Northern Italy	99

ILLUSTRATIONS.

Directions to the Binder.

The Krähmeyer's Cottage . . . . *to face page*	31
The First Lake of Langbath . . . . ,,	38
The Kellnerin . . . . . - ,,	42
Alt-Aussee with the Loser . . . . ,,	47
The First Gosau Lake . . . . ,,	55
Jäger . . . . . ,,	69
Styrian Peasant Woman . . . . ,,	71
Alt-Aussee with the Tresselwand . ,,	125

RAMBLES IN ALPINE LANDS
IN 1863.

I.

(WRITTEN IN 1867.)

It is a popular opinion that the retired Anglo-Indian is the most miserable of human beings. Burying himself in Bayswater,—rightly on that account dignified with the nickname of Asia-Minor,—the old Indian is generally supposed to reserve to himself the right of grumbling at a society in which he does not mingle, and of railing at people to whose customs he is too Indianized to conform. We do not say that this impression is correct, but we do affirm that it is very generally entertained by the English, pure and simple. These have come to regard the great bulk of Anglo-Indians as a race entirely apart, separated from themselves by peculiar ideas upon most subjects, by an incapacity to converse upon other than matters pertaining to India, by a pertinacious exaltation of the customs of Anglo-Indians in India, as compared with those of the English in England. Admitting these impressions to be true as regards the majority of retired Anglo-Indians—of the men who spent thirty years in India without once, in the interval, revisiting their native land,—we believe it will be generally conceded that the nearer and more frequent communication with England, which has been gradually progressing since the establishment of the Overland route, together with reforms consequent on the Mutiny, is bringing about great, and will yet bring about greater, changes in this respect. These changes are indicated by the improvement which has already taken place in the choice of subjects of conversation in Indian society in India itself. Thirty years ago the man that would have made any allusion to English politics at an Indian dinner party would have at once been set down as a prig or a bore. He would have alluded to subjects which, to the remainder of the company present, would have been the veriest Hebrew, with which scarcely one man in a hundred ever troubled himself. The truth of this statement has lately received the fullest confirmation in Miss Eden's amusing account of her travels with Lord Auckland up the country. We there see in what light a clever, well-educated, well-informed English lady regarded the society amongst whose members her lot had been temporarily cast. "Their men," she says, "can talk only about Vizier Ali, and their ladies about nothing at all." We can quite believe that this criticism was perfectly applicable in those days. We can thoroughly understand how Miss Eden, who had mixed in the best society in England, who had been associated with the leaders of English parties, and who had taken a more than ordinary interest in English politics, should have found herself

vexed, and bored, and fatigued to a degree at being forced
to confine herself to a society to the members of which
English politics were a sealed book, and the history of
English parties absolute Chaldee; who had with her not
one subject in common, whose ideas were limited to the
promotion of their husbands, and to their own precedence
at Government House. It may indeed be remarked that
Miss Eden's memoirs relate to a period too remote to be
quoted as in any way illustrating the present epoch. We
perfectly coincide with this objection, but we cannot help
observing at the same time that the late Albert Smith,
himself no ordinary observer of human nature, made, at a
much more recent period, a remark not very dissimilar. It
was the fortune of that popular author to proceed to England from Galle in one of the Overland steamers crammed
full of Anglo-Indians. With respect to the ladies, Albert
Smith remarked that they appeared to be so entirely
engrossed with a struggle for their own precedence
at the dinner-table, that they seemed absolutely unable to
talk of anything else. With regard to men, he observed
that, judging from their conversation during a voyage of
sixteen days, he had come to the conclusion that in their
opinion India was the vastest, the grandest, the most important empire in the globe; that upon the sayings and
doings, upon the promotions and appointments, of every
man in that Indian Empire, the eyes of the entire civilized
world were fixed with the most intense longing; that they
regarded England as a distant island, entirely dependent
upon India, and the only use of which was to supply Anglo-
Indians with beer and cheroots. It is difficult to believe

that this is not an overdrawn picture; but that it was sketched by a man possessing peculiarly observant powers, who had no interest in vilifying Anglo-Indians, or in exposing them to ridicule and contempt, is a clear proof that it had some foundation.

It would be in the highest degree unfair, however, to take this, in even a modified form, as at all an accurate description of Indian society twelve years ago. On boardship many people are peevish, uncertain, and selfish; they display the worst side of their characters. Steamers from India, too, carry a particularly large proportion of invalids, and it can scarcely be wondered at if, deprived of their accustomed luxuries, shut up in small boxes dignified by the name of cabins, crowded together to a most inconvenient degree, these people vent on one another the accumulated bile of many years' Indian existence, and appear to a stranger on board infinitely more disagreeable than they would be, if met under their own punkahs or by their own firesides.

If, then, we may consider Albert Smith's description as overdrawn, applied to the Anglo-Indian of twelve years since, we do not hesitate to assert that we regard it as totally inapplicable to the Anglo-Indians of the present day. Since that period the moral atmosphere of India has been cleared by the thunder-storm of the Mutiny, and the old ideas, which produced the conduct so strongly condemned by Albert Smith, have been replaced by others fresher, more sensible, more consonant to the spirit of the age. Were Miss Eden to reappear on the Indian stage, we are confident that she would not now complain that the men could only talk of Vizier Ali, and the ladies of nothing at all. English politics are not unfrequently discussed in Anglo-Indian society. The characters of the public men of Europe are fairly known, and are freely commented upon. Events of European interest are looked forward to often with an eagerness which may be pronounced intense. There is, within our own experience, infinitely less longing for social precedence than existed before the Mutiny. England is no longer regarded as a dependency of India, to provide it with beer and cheroots, but it is looked upon as the land of promise—the country a return to which before a man's energies are entirely exhausted by this exhausting country, is the temporal aim and object of the life of almost every man. This feeling is re-acting and will re-act still more upon the retired Anglo-Indians at home. We mean that the men who now retire will be different in many respects from their predecessors. It will be their pride to be Englishmen, instead of merely members of a distant colony in the Asia-Minor of Bayswater. They will cease to pronounce the customs of the English inhospitable, and their manners cold and distant. Their frequent visits to England, during their period of service, will teach them that in a country in which it is possible for a pickpocket to wear as good a coat as a peer, it is absolutely necessary that a man should have a special introduction to an English gentleman, before this last will associate with him on terms of equality and confidence; that it is not sufficient, as some old Indians of the present day imagine, that a man should have been Commissioner, or a Colonel, or a Sudder Judge, in order to be accepted as a great man by Englishmen, receiving the same respect and adulation from the masses as would be readily accorded to the holders of such positions in India. They will find out before very many months, that in England a man is received and treated, not with reference to the appointments he has held in this country, but simply and solely according to the manner in which he conducts himself at home. A man who is clever, well-informed, *au courant* with all the events of the day, will find himself a welcome guest in any society. In such a case, the Anglo-Indian will find that the fact of having spent many years of his life in this country operates often as a point in his favour. It is only when Anglo-Indians are pompous, opiniative, hankering after positions which they cannot attain, intolerant of others, and openly expressing a longing for the fleshpots they have left—and this is now the character they have earned in England—that they find their service in India acts in the minds of ordinary men to their prejudice.

But that the younger members of the Anglo-Indian community will fall into the errors, in this respect, of their predecessors, we consider more than improbable. Every day shows us how all the un-English habits of the Anglo-Indian are one after another being cast aside; how the rage for precedence has disappeared; how the assumption of airs and graces by an individual, who may happen to possess some high office in the State, has come to be regarded, even by the services, as eminently ridiculous; how the toleration of the opinion of others is, save by a remnant of the old leaven, looked upon as a matter of course. In fact, we may sum up our review of the progress of Anglo-Indian society since the Mutiny by this simple remark; that it has been a gradual and increasing progress towards the state of society in England.

Nothing has tended more to bring about this improved order of things, than the increased facility of communication with Europe, and the opening out of new routes to the traveller. Of these in the present day there is an almost unlimited choice. From Alexandria steamers leave, in connection with the Indian steamers, for all parts of the world. There is the time-honoured route to England by Southampton,—the best probably for invalids,—and the almost equally well-worn course by Marseilles. Of the older routes, too, Trieste puts in a well-considered claim for patronage. Amongst those more recently opened out, too, are Ancona and Brindisi. The latter bids fair to usurp the place of Marseilles, so far as relates to the carriage of the mails. But the lover of the picturesque will never choose wittingly the route by Brindisi. The long dreary railway journey from that place to Ancona presents nothing to please or delight the eye. Far preferable, and scarcely longer, would be the route from Malta to Naples, thence by Rome, Florence, and Milan, to the Italian lakes. From Milan there is a profuse choice of routes homewards, in the selection of which the traveller will follow his own tastes. Our own predilection we decline even distantly to hint at. We are free however to admit that the perusal of the unpublished journal which we propose to analyse in this article, has convinced us that an Indian traveller may experience intense delight and enjoyment, when pursuing, with a light heart and taste not too vitiated by long years of sojourn in India, a route so well known and so well worn as is that of Trieste.

Captain Musafir* would appear to be an officer of the Bengal army, who left India with his wife some four or five years ago on twenty months' sick leave to Europe. What has since become of him we are unable to state, nor indeed is it necessary to our story. His journal was handed over to us with the most satisfactory proofs as to its authenticity. Of this indeed it bears undoubted internal evidence, and it is this alone which makes it valuable. We gather from a few prefatory remarks affixed to it that Musafir was a fair German scholar, a great lover of the picturesque, an adventurous traveller, and an ardent devotee of "the gentle art." His predilection indeed for this harmless sport appears to have been confirmed and strengthened by the notorious fact that the trout and grayling always choose their habitation in those rivers which meander through the loveliest valleys, and which are fed by streamlets from the grandest and most magnificent mountains. His taste for the picturesque and his love of travelling would seem to have been shared by his wife, for it is evident from the journal that she accompanied him everywhere, and found that the glorious scenery to which she was transported far more than compensated for the rough accommodation, by submitting to which a view of such scenery was often alone attainable.

We gather from the journal that after the ordinary inci-

---

* "Musafir" is the Persian for traveller.

dents of an overland voyage, our two travellers arrived at Trieste at 11 o'clock on the 15th May.* They put up at the Hotel de la Ville, which they describe as being one of the best and most luxurious hotels on the Continent, being furnished with hot and cold baths, and every possible convenience. It is, however, dear in comparison with hotels in other parts of the Continent. This arises from the fact that Trieste itself is a very expensive city. Attached to the Austrian Empire, it is yet a free port, and in possession of this privilege it has attained to a degree of prosperity which fairly takes the traveller by surprise. The shops are numerous and well stocked; the equipages well built and remarkably well-horsed; the ladies elegantly and handsomely dressed. The promenades are crowded, whilst the poorer people seem to wear a happy and contented air, and to be full of employment. There are two opera-houses besides theatres and other places of amusement. The houses are well built and comfortable, with handsome exteriors. There is an abundance of pretty villas along the shores of the Adriatic and on the hills behind the town. In fact, in whatever direction the traveller may turn, he meets striking evidences of a prosperous, well-ordered, and contented community.

Our travellers were much struck with the appearance of the town and its inhabitants. Musafir records, how even at the hotel door he and his wife were met by flower-

---

* The date of the year is not given in any part of the journal, but from the state of completion of the railways, it could not have been more than five or six years ago, possibly less.

girls carrying with them the loveliest flowers, which, either singly or made up into bouquets, they almost force upon the traveller. Few of these refuse the proffered gift, or fail to return it by a present of some small coins. But should they refuse, they are deprived of the extreme pleasure of hearing, probably for the first time in their lives, in the melodious tones and soft accents of Italy, and delivered as if coming from the heart, the sweet sounding *Grazie*. Of the houses and villas along the shores of the Adriatic to which we have alluded, certainly the most striking is the palace of Miramare, lately the residence of the Archduke Maximilian, brother of the Emperor of Austria, and now himself Emperor of Mexico. A good view of this palace can be obtained from Trieste itself, for it stands on a tongue of land jutting out into the Adriatic, thus seeming, from a short distance, to be as it were detached from the main land. It is the point which first strikes every traveller after his arrival. Musafir and his wife were not content with a distant view of it, but drove out with some friends to inspect it. It is distant from Trieste about five miles, and the road to it borders the Adriatic on the one side, whilst a range of high hills on the other, clad with rich verdure, presents a striking contrast to the deep blue of the sea. The palace itself is built in the real Gothic style, and is most beautiful. Only a portion of the interior was visible, as the Archduke and Archduchess were residing there at the time; but that portion showed how completely comfort had been united with elegance in the construction. The gardens attached to it have been beautifully laid out. The ground from the castle ascends, and of this ascent every possible advantage has been taken. There are natural grottos cut out of the rock, arbours ingeniously formed so as to command the loveliest view and to be impervious to the brightest sun. The flowers are luxuriant, their beds arranged with great taste and kept in the most perfect order. The whole garden, in fact, presented the appearance of a fairy land, culminating in the enchanting castle on the sea. The Archduke and Archduchess generally stroll about the grounds in the afternoon, mingling freely with the people to whom they courteously allow admittance. On the evening, however, our travellers visited it, they did not appear.

To obtain entrance into the grounds it was simply necessary for Musafir to present his card. The tall, soldierly lodge-keeper who demanded it, had all the appearance of a man who had seen military service, and Musafir could not help putting the question to him when the party went out. He replied, records Musafir, in the following words: "Yes, I have served, but it was in Hungary and against Austria." He added in a proud, melancholy tone, "I am a Hungarian." It appeared from further questioning that he had served under Bem, and had fought as long as any hope remained for Hungary; that after Russian soldiers had trampled out the last spark of the fight for freedom, he had taken a civil post. With the Archduke he had been for the past six years. His connection with the Imperial House had not, however, changed his sympathies at all; for when Musafir enquired from him whether he did not think that an union between the two countries with one parliament for both would not satisfy all legitimate aspirations, he replied in a tone the mournfulness of which, writes Musafir, it would be impossible to describe: "It would be beneficial for Austria, but not for Hungary." It was curious to hear this expression of genuine patriotism, uttered in despotic Austria, and at the gates of the palace of an Austrian Archduke!

We have alluded to the hills behind Trieste. These are extremely pretty and abound in drives presenting glorious views of the Adriatic. On the day following their visit to Miramare our travellers drove to a village called Sessana, on the line of the Vienna railway. Sessana is nothing in itself, but the drive to it is most lovely. The road winds up a gradual ascent of 1,800 feet, and commands, during its course, after the first half-hour, a splendid view of Trieste, the Adriatic, and of the picturesque town of Pirano on the Illyrian coast. On a very clear day, free from haze, Venice may be seen. At Sessana, our travellers met an Austrian officer, a native of the province of Moravia, who had served in the Italian campaign of 1859, regarding which he conversed freely. He did ample justice to the French soldiers and their emperor. Of the latter indeed he said that if he had been at the head of the Austrian army and if Giulay had commanded the French, he was confident victory would have been with the Austrians. Their defeat at Magenta he attributed to the utter incompetence of Giulay, and their ill-success in the campaign to the treachery and disaffection of the Hungarian and Italian regiments. He appeared most anxious for a fresh trial. "Let the Emperor," he said, "send to Italy only Moravians, Bohemians, Croats and Austrians, and let him place Benedek at their head, and, I'll answer for it, we'll win back Italy." It appears from various entries in the journal that this feeling was shared by almost all the Austrian officers and privates our travellers met with.

On their return to Trieste the travellers followed another and more circuitous road, in order to visit the Imperial breeding stud at Lipizza,—a place famous for its grass lands. The sight here was well worth seeing. At Lipizza there are horses of all nations, amongst them many English thoroughbreds. But those that most attracted notice were the Arabs —far more perfect in shape than any Musafir had seen in India. Many of them must have been of the purest Arabian blood, so absolutely faultless was their conformation. The care bestowed on these horses, as well as on the mares and foals, cannot be exceeded. It is a pretty sight to see them loose in their large, well-built houses, all herded together, living in the most perfect amity. They are treated with affection and gentleness by their attendants. No other mode of treatment indeed could have produced the sweet temper and docility displayed by all the animals in this vast establishment.

It is impossible to leave Trieste without alluding to the custom there prevailing, so admirably adapted to a warm climate, of taking enjoyment in the open air. No sooner does the afternoon sun show an inclination to hide his glories behind the not too distant hills, than in front of every *café* numberless chairs and small tables are placed. To these, after the promenade, all Trieste repairs. A band as if by magic appears, and under the vaulted canopy of heaven, the tideless Adriatic at their feet, the honest burghers sip their coffee, enjoy their ices, and listen to the soft music. Occasionally the scene is enlivened by songs from strolling performers. There is no excess, no drunkenness, no uproar. All is conducted with the decorum which rules over the arrangements of a private concert in England. Yet in Trieste this takes place daily, and the sole payment received by the musicians and singers depends on the charity of the listeners. Such a scene would always strike Englishmen; but upon Musafir and his wife, coming as they did from a country hotter than Trieste, but into which the conquering race has introduced the social manners and customs of a northern climate,—the heavy dinners, the formal visits, the tedious drives,—the impression appears to have been most vivid and pleasing.

On the 18th May our travellers left Trieste by railway for Adelsberg, famous for its caves. The line of rail lay among the hills, and the many bends it made, and their sharpness,—sometimes almost at right angles,—appeared to have completely astonished the two Anglo-Indians. The journey itself takes little more than an hour. Adelsberg lies about 1,800 feet above Trieste, and is proportionately cooler. It is in itself but a small village, deriving all its importance from the wonderful caves in its vicinity. To inspect these was the object not only of Musafir and his wife, but of all the travellers who stop at Adelsberg. In order to see the caves in perfection, it is necessary that they should be thoroughly well lighted-up with torches and candles. Our travellers were fortunate enough on their arrival to find that orders for an extraordinary illumination had been issued by some American gentlemen who were staying at the inn, and who permitted them to join their party. Snatching a hasty meal, the whole party left the inn about 11, and arrived at the entrance of the caves a quarter of an hour later. They did not emerge till 3 o'clock. To describe accurately what they saw in that interval would require a paper by itself. Transported suddenly from the fresh, balmy, sunny air of the outside world into the very heart of the earth,—a gloomy cavern with no light save that afforded by the torches of the guides, —the travellers found themselves entering, now vast halls vaulted by rocks and supported seemingly by pillars of alabaster,—now narrow passages the flinty sides of which sparkled like diamonds. Again, they entered the nave of a glorious cathedral, at the other end of which, in the place where the altar should be, was a visible representation of the crucifixion, not carved, but formed naturally by the rock. The grandeur and dread peculiarity of the sight impressed itself on all the members of the party. They could scarcely resist the conviction that they were in another world. Sometimes depressing them by its gloominess, at others exalting them into enthusiasm by the glorious shapes formed by the alabaster-like stalactites, the effect was to make them utterly forgetful of the sun and the trees, the light and the air, the green meads and the running streams they had left outside, and to induce the idea that they were really passing through the valley of the shadow of death, to the vale that led down to the Styx. The apparition of Charon and his boat would not, in those moments, have surprised any of the party. As if to complete the illusion, there was, below them, a river dark as Erebus, flowing onwards through the depths of the earth, and seeming to indicate that there was a point yet to be reached, at which its stream would widen, and interpose a barrier between the visitors and the world beyond. Until the travellers approached the very last of the caves the spell was complete, nor did it leave them till, at a sudden turn, a flood of light reminded them that—

> The earth hath wonders, as the water hath,
> And these are of them!

Leaving Adelsberg the following morning about 9 o'clock, our travellers left for Gratz, the capital of Styria, and arrived there about half-past four the same afternoon. The train carried them through a lovely country. Between Steinbrück and Gratz the alternations of hill and dale were charming. The river Save, between Laibach and Steinbrück, had all the appearance of a good trout river, but there was no stopping to try it. Probably, in common with all the rivers on the line of railway in Austria, it is strictly preserved, the trout being periodically caught and sent up alive in wooden barrels filled with water to Vienna and other large towns, bought up there by the innkeepers, and preserved by them in reservoirs for their customers.

At Gratz our travellers put up at the Archduke John hotel, kept by a most obliging landlord, but one who knew how to charge those travellers who are unacquainted with the German language. To this subject reference will be made further on. Gratz itself is a charming town, very clean, and containing much that is interesting to the traveller. The walks in and about it are most enticing.

Right in the centre of the town rises the Schlossberg, on the summit of which there was once a fort. It now, however, constitutes one of the promenades of the place, and is in every respect well worthy of a visit. The views which it commands of many miles of lovely country in Styria—the most unintermittently beautiful province of the Empire—make the traveller long to set off at once to examine for himself. Indeed, if a tour off the line of rail be the object of the traveller, there are few places better fitted to make a start from than Gratz. Everything is procurable there—horses, mules, carriages, guides, as well as every requisite in the way of clothing for the pedestrian or the ordinary traveller. It is, besides, comparatively a very cheap place. The landlord of the Archduke John assured our travellers that for £150 a year a man and his wife could live very comfortably, and for double that sum like princes. It is this cheapness that has caused Gratz to be selected by most of the retired officers of the Austrian army as their place of residence. Many of these men have but £60 a year. Gratz, moreover, has many other advantages. It has an excellent and very cheap club, frequented chiefly by military men; capital public reading-rooms; it is very healthy, and has very good theatres. The military bands play out constantly. It forms, moreover, the southern gate, as Linz is the northern, into the very loveliest part of Austria—a country which, it is to be hoped, may long remain closed to the mere tourist, open only to the adventurous lover of the picturesque.

The town itself is divided into two parts by the river Mûr, very rapid in its course, with turbid, discoloured waters. It supplies the town with coarse fish in abundance, and in the winter with the huchen (*salmo hucro*), the German salmon. In the neighbourhood, the sights usually visited by those whose stay there is limited are Maria Trost, Maria Grün, and the Hilmer Teich. The first of these is a church and monastery, beautifully situated on the summit of a hill, some five miles from Gratz. The church is picturesque from a distance, but contains nothing within it worthy of much notice. The view, however, from it is glorious. On the one side Gratz itself, looking extremely pretty, embosomed in the green hills and cut in twain by the rapid Mûr, on the other the splendid range of the Styrian Alps, height piled on height, tempting, sorely tempting to the pedestrian. The walk from Maria Trost to Maria Grün, is very lovely, leading the traveller, as the name signifies, to the most beautiful foliage. On the grassy beds wild flowers in great and beautiful variety are abundant. At the place itself is a small chapel of no great significance, but the walks all about it are most enticing. The Hilmer Teich is a large pond or lake full of tame carp, very prettily situated in grounds on a hill which slopes upwards from the pond. Both pond and grounds are kept most carefully. This is the great afternoon resort of the beauty and fashion of Gratz.* Here, while a

---

* The people of Gratz are very agreeable to strangers. Towards their own Government they assume a free and independent bearing, quite new to the traveller who has heard of nothing but despotism in connexion with Austria. Here assembles the provincial diet of Styria, the resolutions of which are not always pleasing to the Austrian Emperor. Though almost all the inhabitants are Catholic, all religions are tolerated, and there is a Protestant church in the town.

splendid band does justice even to the genius of the great German composers, they sip their coffee, row on the lake, or stroll about the pretty grounds. As the ladies of Gratz dress well and with great taste, the sight to a stranger cannot fail to be attractive.

The Musafirs left Gratz unwillingly on the morning of the 23rd May. The bowing landlord of the Archduke John presented them with a bill which, though not moderate, could scarcely be called excessive; yet their respect for him on that account diminished considerably when they learned that he had charged three English ladies, who had stayed at his hotel only half the time, nearly double the sum. The reason, the Musafirs ascertained, was that these ladies were ignorant of German. Their further experience in Austria proved to them that a knowledge of the German language, by at least one of the party, was essential to economical travelling; and even very often to comfort. Such knowledge implies the knowledge likewise of the customs of the country; and the landlords, anxious as they are to take every advantage of English travellers, are afraid to impose upon them too much under such circumstances. In their after journey, the Musafirs heard repeatedly of English travellers who had paid double and treble the price charged to them for the very same accommodation and for similar meals.

The rail from Gratz to Brück follows the course of the troubled and turbid Mûr. At Brück, however, another river, the Mürz, joined in, of a very different character. As far as Mürz-zu-schlag, this clear bright river gladdened the eyes of the travellers, running through a smiling country, inviting a further inspection and a lengthened visit. At

Mürz-zu-schlag they commenced the ascent of the Semmering, the road across which was then regarded as one of the greatest engineering triumphs ever accomplished. The scenery over this pass is extremely grand.

About 4 o'clock that same afternoon, our travellers reached Vienna, and put up at the Kaiserin Elisabeth, a clean and comfortable hotel. Vienna is too well known, and has been too often described, to need any reference to it in this sketch. It will suffice to remark that the Musafirs appear to have been less struck with the city than they expected, but to have been remarkably impressed with the light, gay, and jovial character of the people, and with the extreme politeness of the officials. It happened to fall to the lot of Musafir to call on the Minister of Police to request a slight favour. This gentleman not only readily granted it, but, when Musafir left the room, he, a Baron of the Empire, insisted on rising and conducting him to the door. Nothing, in fact, could exceed the civility they met with from the officers of the Government on all occasions but one.

It being the object of the Musafirs to make a lengthened tour in that lovely part of the country known as the Salzkammergut, and in the Austrian and Bavarian Alps, it formed no part of their plan to remain long in any city, however attractive, and they accordingly left Vienna on the afternoon of the fourth day after their arrival, and proceeded by train to Linz—a town before alluded to as the northern gate of the lovely mountainous regions of Austria. There is an alternate route to that by rail, namely the steam-trip up the Danube, and that many travellers would doubtless prefer. From Vienna to Linz, however, by the Danube route, involved in those days the necessity of sleeping one night on board a steamer. The finest part of the river, moreover, is between Linz and Passau, a river-trip of but nine hours, and our travellers resolved therefore upon proceeding to Linz by rail, thence inspecting the Danube by a trip from that place to Passau, then returning to Linz, and from it to enter the much celebrated Salzkammergut.

Linz, which they reached by rail that same evening, is charmingly situated on the Danube. To the north and east of it picturesque hills rise moderately to add to its beauty, whilst, stretching out south and west, may be seen the hills and mountains of the Salzkammergut, and beyond them the giant ranges of the Noric Alps, magnificent with their snow-capped heights. The view from the smaller hills first alluded to is extremely beautiful, and though not perhaps so soft and regular as that from the Schlossberg or Maria Trost at Gratz, yet the superiority of the mighty Danube to the turbid Mûr gave this, in the eyes of Musafir, a greater charm. The sight alone of this splendid river, separating into several channels, then moving grandly and imposingly along, at once rivets the attention and invites admiration. Then, again, at right angles to it, about a mile below the town of Linz, may be seen running into it a little river, tumbling among rocks, rapid in its course, bright green in its colour—a river which from its appearance thrills the heart of the fisherman. This river is the famous Traun, the artery of the Salzkammergut; the guide to the finest scenery, in many respects, in the world. Hail to thee, thou shining stream; all hail to further acquaintance with thy bright waters!

Linz itself is a clean town; but in the extent of its resources it cannot be compared to Gratz. The shops are inferior, it is less populated, and the better class are evidently poorer. The fact is that the Linzers have had to strive against a great many difficulties. They have had to pay for the construction of a series of round underground forts, built on a system invented by the late Archduke Maximilian of Este—and which, comparing land with sea fortifications, may be said to approach more nearly to the turret-system than any other. These forts are in fact underground turrets, presenting nothing for an enemy to fire at, and yet capable of pouring forth a continuous and destructive fire on an advancing enemy. They have hitherto been untried in actual warfare, but there is little doubt but that they would be useful if they enclosed sufficient space to accommodate within the circle they embraced a large army, which would then occupy, as it were, an intrenched camp. But, in the case of the fortifications of Linz, this result is not obtained. There is not space enough within the circle comprehended by Maximilian's forts to contain a large army; whilst the small one which that circle could contain might be easily held in check by a small hostile army, leaving the main body of the enemy to march on Vienna. All this is recognized by the unfortunate Linzers, who have the poor consolation of feeling that they have been taxed heavily for fortifications which are practically useless, and that they have still to pay five per cent. on the unliquidated portion of the debt due on account of them. Whilst the Musafirs were at Linz intelligence arrived of the death of the inventive Archduke.

It is almost impossible to describe the feeling of intense relief produced by this news, inasmuch as, only very shortly before, Maximilian believed he had invented a new and improved system, and he had proposed to bring this into operation at the expense of the burghers of Linz. His death, therefore, was hailed as an exemption from further taxation.

It is the fashion to look upon the Austrians as a race sunk into the deepest depths of moral and political degradation, but travellers like Musafir and his wife will probably draw a very different conclusion. In the first place, absolute poverty appeared unknown. The men, who earned their bread by the sweat of their brows, occupied cottages which were decent-looking outside and comfortable within. It is, besides, a note-worthy fact, that of these pretty-looking cottages there was not one the windows of which were not filled with flowers—a circumstance insignificant, perhaps, in itself, but which appears to indicate contentment and refined taste on the part of the poorer population.

Sunday at Linz is a very gay day. Between 8 and 9 o'clock in the morning the petty shop-keepers and peasants, decked out in their best, with their mass-books under their arms, may be seen wending their way from the other side of the Danube, across the bridge, to the church, the toning of whose bells reminded all of the day of rest from toil. Two hours later all Linz was promenading in the pretty avenue near the theatre. In such a lovely climate, with the bright hot days, natural to the country, everything seemed to invite to a walk in the open air. There was no artificial gloom, no constraint, no gin-shop quarrels, no enforced penalty for being happy. The people went quietly and decorously to worship God in the morning, and enjoyed afterwards the blessings of His Providence in the glorious sunshine. The shops were all shut, with the exception of those for the sale of provisions. Those who have witnessed the hot dinners served out to the poor in England on Sunday, need not impute this as a crime to the honest Linzers. There is a Protestant church, the service at which our travellers attended; but the account they gave of it was by no means favourable.

One of the prettiest views obtainable at Linz is that from the top of the hill called the Pöstlingberg, commanding a splendid view of the surrounding country. The many channels of the Danube and the windings of the bright green Traun, in the foreground, with the Alps stretching far back as the eye could reach, made the landscape a glorious one. It was impossible for our travellers to resist the impression that this was indeed the Pisgah of the beautiful country of which they had heard so much.

At Linz, where they stayed at the Rother Krebs, a most comfortable hotel on the Danube, Musafir and his wife were joined by two Australian fellow-passengers who, partly on their recommendation, had come to explore the beauties of Austria. These gentlemen, even during the voyage, had betrayed some curiosity with respect to a little paragraph which appears in Murray's "Hand-book for Southern Germany," in which reference is made to the surpassing beauty of the ladies of Passau. They resolved, therefore, to join Musafir and his wife in their contemplated visit to that city. On the morning of the 29th May, accordingly, the four started in the steamer. The scenery for the greater part of the way, more especially between Aschach and Passau, they found strikingly grand and magnificent. The grandeur, too, was derived entirely from nature. There is little artificial about the Danube. Here and there, indeed, a ruin, or a modern castle, adds interest to the scene. But, on the whole, Nature alone has designed and painted the picture. But not in this respect alone does it differ from the Rhine. The banks of the latter are varied by towns, inland scenery, castles, châteaux, and the river is everywhere bustling with life. Its surface is covered with steamers, rafts, boats, and pleasure parties. On the Danube, on the contrary, all is calm and serenely beautiful. But few villages, three or four castles, perhaps only one steamer, and not half-a-dozen rafts, meet the eye in the course of the day. The course of the steamer lies between high hills covered with green verdure, the varied tints of which are charming. Round and through these the river winds and twists. Of life, however, there is little. Whilst, therefore, the Danube would more interest the enthusiastic lover of nature, the Rhine would in all probability more attract the general traveller.

The view of Passau from the Danube is most striking. The traveller comes first upon the suburb of Innstadt on the Inn, then on the city itself—on a central point of land between the Inn and the Danube—and lastly on the black little stream,—the Ilz,—the Ilzstadt suburb hanging over it. The *coup d'œil* is quite charming, whilst the green hills behind the town and its suburbs add to the serenity and beauty of the scene.

4

Passau itself strikingly reminds the traveller of a city that has been. The buildings in the old town are very fine, but are almost entirely void of inhabitants. Even the hotel at which our travellers stopped had a gloomy and deserted appearance, and the very ancient waiter in his long grey coat seemed to belong rather to the 17th than to the 19th century. This man was a character in his way. He told Musafir that he was a rigid Catholic, and he lamented that the English were not so likewise. It was all owing, he said, to that "teufel" King Henry *the* 4*th* "who had cut off the heads of Queen Charlotte Corday, and of nine other wives on account of their Catholicism!"

But of all the disappointments in store for the visitors to Passau, the greatest was experienced by the Australian explorers of pretty faces. In vain did they search the streets, the churches, the markets, the thoroughfares—not one even tolerably good-looking woman was to be seen. The shop of the principal photographer was examined with a similar result. The artist frankly declared that it had never been his good fortune to be sat to by a beauty. Great was the indignation of the explorers; the youngest was even heard to mutter something about an action against Mr. Murray for misdescription. Even he, however, soon calmed down. He could not be for long insensible to the extreme beauty of the locality. That indeed was more than sufficient to compensate for the other disappointment. The walk from Passau to Hals, a ruined castle on the black Ilz, was quite charming; nor could one regard without interest the waters of the three rivers, so different in colour, flowing on as far as the eye could reach without intermingling. Our travellers were not sorry, however, to return the same evening to Linz, the streets of which appeared bright and gay in comparison with Passau. Here they remained for the Sunday, then started on the following morning for their tour in the Salzkammergut.

This lovely province of Austria, so called from its constituting the great salt district of the Empire, is entered by Linz on the north, and is bounded on the west by Salzburg, on the south by the Styrian and Noric ranges, including the snow-topped Dachstein, and on the east by Styria itself. It is a land of mountains, of lakes, and of rivers; of trout and of chamois; of brave men and fair women; of a people who are simple-hearted and honest, active, enduring, courteous to strangers, given to hospitality. A finer race there is not in the world than these hardy sons and honest-hearted daughters of Austria. They are, too, a stalwart, well-set up, well-formed people, God-fearing yet merry, hardworking yet never sulky or morose. Joy is in all their dwellings,—a joy unstimulated by excess, and untainted by vice: it is to them quite natural. Poor they may be, but they feel none of the ills of poverty. Their own fair land produces for them in abundance and to spare. They toil, however, yet right merrily, and it is no uncommon practice to see the peasants of both sexes assemble on the green sward after the day's work is over, and dance, to their hearts' content, the pretty national dances of Styria and Upper Austria.

Our travellers proceeded from Linz as far as Lambach by rail, then alighted in order to enjoy the lovely drive from Lambach to Gmunden, and to visit the falls of the

Traun, about midway between the two places. Lambach itself is prettily situated on the green Traun, and is a neat little town, commanding a fine view of the distant mountains. It boasts of a decent little inn, the Black Horse, the landlord of which had just returned from a visit to England, immensely struck with the degree of high pressure in farming there attained. He was himself a farmer in a fair way, and had some capital stock in his stables,—the produce of Hungarian blood. The prices he had given for some of these were ludicrously small. For a fine-looking, well-boned, strong-backed horse about sixteen hands high, stepping like a park-horse, he named £16 or £17 as the price he had paid. His Hungarian pigs, too, were remarkably fine, but as fierce as wild boars, and disdaining in appearance all relationship with the animal as known in England.

Lambach is well worthy of a longer visit than our travellers paid it. They, for instance, had no time to visit the Benedictine monastery hanging over the Traun, famous for its library. To the good monks belongs the exclusive right of fishing in that river as far as the falls, and they freely accorded it to Musafir. The distant view of the mountain range was, however, too seducing, and he hastened to push on. The second day after their arrival, therefore, they started in a nice, easy carriage, drawn by a pair of their landlord's best horses, for Gmunden. The drive, somewhat under two hours, was most lovely, the day was fine, and the scenery as bright and varied as scenery could be. Before them were the lofty mountains, approaching ever nearer and nearer, some of them peaked with snow, others with patches of it on their bluff fronts,—one quite covered, a huge mass of shining white. On either side of them were, now a forest of tall pines, now undulating green fields, sometimes the swiftly-flowing Traun. At the end of an hour the Traun falls are reached, and these they descended to examine. How to describe the undescribable! The mass of water, the foam of spray, the rocks standing immoveable in the midst, the lovely scenery on the high steep bank,—all combined to make up a picture, which if not in the strict sense of the word grand, is still intensely beautiful. To those, perhaps, who have seen the great falls of America, or even the Rhine fall at Schaffhausen, the Traun falls will doubtless appear, as falls, tame in comparison, but from the lover of beautiful scenery they must always evoke the admiration which their unique and simple beauty deserves.

Gmunden itself, which was reached some forty minutes later, is a lovely spot. The lake itself, nine miles long, with clear, deep water through which the Traun takes its course, and with mountains rising, as it were, from its very deepest depths to an overpowering height above it, is most glorious. Midway down its banks, opposite the giant Traunstein, is the little village of Traunkirchen, most picturesquely situated, and containing one comfortable little inn,—the best place for the traveller to stop in. The view from the windows of this inn is lovely, and never tiring. The water is full of life, covered with steamers plying between Gmunden and Ebensee, with pleasure boats, with fishing-boats, the giant Traunstein behind them all, the waters dark in his shadow. The banks of the lake and the small elevations near it are covered with little villas deliciously inviting for a summer residence. Most of these belong to the Austrian aristocracy, who use them for that purpose, preferring Gmunden, with its lake, to the court-frequented Ischl which has only the Traun. Living at Gmunden is decidedly cheap. At the Golden Sun, where our travellers stopped, they were charged seven shillings for a bedroom and dinner including beer. Even then the honest landlady apologised for charging so much, " but," she said, " trout are half-a-crown the pound."

As mention has been made of beer, it may be observed that all over the Salzkammergut that agreeable and often necessary stimulant is to be had in great perfection. There are two places, however, where it is pre-eminently excellent, unsurpassable by any ale that Burton can produce. One of these is the town of Wels, between Lambach and Gmunden. The beer here is most undeniable. The brewer supplies most, but not all, of the inns at Gmunden. The other place is the city of Salzburg. The beer here obtainable is called the Kaltenhausen, from the name of the brewery in the vicinity, the property of Count Arco, a famous Bavarian sportsman. This beer surpasses even that of Wels; but it must be specially called for if required. Mr. Jung, the excellent landlord of the Hotel de l'Europe at Salzburg, to whom we hope our readers will be introduced some day, always keeps a supply of it. Its admirers say, and say truly, that it is " better than champagne."

After a stay of a day or two at Gmunden, the Musafirs proceeding by steamer to Ebensee, the southern end of the lake, left the high road to make a more lengthened stay near the little lakes of Langbath, two gems embosomed in the heart of the most lovely country possible to conceive. The village of Langbath forms, with that of Ebensee, the southern extremity of the lake of Gmunden. Five miles from this, up a gradual descent through a beautiful and hilly country, on the banks of a little trout-stream, one of the feeders of the Traun, is a little dwelling-place, half inn, half farmhouse, called the Krähe, owned by a man named Loidl, but generally known in the district, from his ownership of the Krähe, as the Krähmeyer. This Krähmeyer is a very fine fellow. Stong-built, active, good-humoured, he was accounted, till within the last few years, the best climber and the most daring mountaineer in Austria. He could almost run up some of the mountains which surround his comfortable little dwelling. No toil was too great, no journey too long or too venturesome that he should refuse to undertake it. Before the game-laws were made as strict as they now are in Austria, it is said that chamois venison was ever plentiful at the Krähe; the flesh of the roebuck and the lordly stag were always too at the service of the guests of the Krähmeyer. But time has changed all this now. The daring cragsman has seen at least his fiftieth summer, and he is content to leave to others the perils of the chase. Never now does he even attempt the ascent of a mountain. He is still, however, a splendid specimen of a man. Honest, good-humoured, content with his lot, satisfied now with fishing the lakes instead of climbing the mountain, with driving where he would before have walked, he is yet ever ready to assist his guests in any expedition they may make, to smooth difficulties, to pilot them on the lakes, or to procure guides for them up the mountains. His wife is his worthy partner. A good-natured, motherly old lady; always looking after the comforts of others, simple-minded, unselfish, and—what is of no small importance—a very fair cook in her way. The little house, now owned by them for many years, is charmingly situated on a grassy spot, surrounded by forest and mountain, some of these covered with snow. The view from this cottage is in itself invigorating; it is so picturesque, so full of the beauties of nature, so health-imparting. In front of the inn is a little garden, planted with trees under which are chairs and tables, and at these most travellers dine. Below this is the little river which has been followed from Ebensee, and which here, close to the inn, tumbles over the rock with foam and roar, and forms a splendid *douche* bath. The basin into which it tumbles is some ten or twelve feet deep; the water bright, clear, and cold. The luxury of a plunge into this after a hard day's work is not to be described. The good old hostess, perhaps, will warn you against the coldness of the water; but, if you are an Englishman, such warning is given in vain. To go to the bank—where you are sheltered from outer view—to strip, to plunge in, is the work of but two minutes. The enjoyment is not to be described; still less the feeling of freshness, of freedom from lassitude, of anxiety to start at once on fresh expeditions, which follow the immersion.

But we have said nothing of the little lakes—the gems which our travellers came to see. The first is distant from the Krähe about three-quarters of a mile. The walk to it is most lovely. Starting through flowery meads, which form

ANATOMY OF VIRUS

THE FIRST LANGRAYR LAKE.

a beautiful foreground to the mountains towering above, the traveller soon enters a glorious wood, into which the sun itself cannot penetrate. Through this, however, is a beautiful path which he follows, till emerging from the wood he comes into a park-like avenue, with trees and shrubs on either side. Turning a corner he finds himself suddenly in the presence of the first lake. It is not very large, perhaps nearly a mile long and about as broad—but it is very beautiful. On its right, the thickly-planted forest down to the water's edge, seemingly impenetrable—the trees covering the bank, which rises high above the surface; on the left, more open, yet still covered with trees, is a kind of wood, through which runs the pathway along the edge of the lake; on the other side, a grassy foreground, on which is erected a small shooting box, the property of the emperor; behind that a magnificent forest of lofty trees; behind that again, and indeed all around, the glorious mountains. It is a soft yet beautiful sight; the calm surface of the deep lake setting off the scenery around it, and intensifying by its own bright beauty the loveliness of the scene.

That is the first lake. Crossing it in a little canoe, of which there are plenty belonging to the Krähmeyer, the traveller jumps on the grassy plot alluded to, passes by the Emperor's shooting-box, and enters the forest. The trees in this are remarkable for their stately loftiness. The walk through them has a romantic wildness about it, in striking contrast with the pleasant brightness on the other side of the first lake. After walking for a good mile and a half, the sound of rushing water strikes upon the ear, and the traveller finds himself close to the little rivulet which drains the lake. Then, all at once, a corner is turned, and the little lake itself, the gem of the district, is before him.

It is very small, smaller than the first lake. But both sides of it are beautifully wooded. Its real grandeur, however, is caused by a solid mass of light grey, almost white, rock, which, stretching on either side far beyond the lake, seems to rise almost perpendicularly to a height of upwards of four thousand feet, from its further end. This rock seems too steep to climb, yet it is swarming with chamois, and is, in fact, one of the favourite haunts of the Kaiser. Gazing at it from the opposite side, its stupendous form assumes the shape of two ruined castles frowning down upon the lake. The combination is perfect. The clear water of the lake—assuming, however, every moment different hues from the shadows cast upon it,—the luxurious foliage, the stately castellated rocks, form a *tout ensemble* which perfectly rivets the attention. Far grander is this than the first lake, beautiful as that is; far more calculated to strike the imagination, to absorb one's whole faculties. One could remain for hours and gaze at this most lovely scene, going the circuit of the lake, or venturing on the surface of its deep waters, gaining from each move a peep into some new beauty. To see that alone a journey from India would not be thrown away.

It was this locality—this little inn and these two lakes—which Musafir and his wife selected for their first halting-place in the Salzkammergut. Eight days did they remain here, and they were eight days of the most perfect enjoyment. Always out of doors, now making an excursion to the lakes, now to the mountains, now rambling through the woods,

now rowing over the lakes, attempting vainly sometimes to
explore their very depths, their time passed pleasantly and
quickly away. It seemed to be the one care of the good
old couple at the inn to make their English guests as com-
fortable as possible. There were, besides, two Germans
residing there,—one an Austrian who had been a great deal
in England; the other a Bohemian,—a retired officer, and a
first-rate mountaineer. The great passion of these two
gentlemen, however, was fishing. They made their own rods
and their own tackle in a style which London would not have
disdained, and they were most successful in extracting
the spotted trout and the silver charr from both the lakes.
Most friendly genial fellows they were. One, alas! died
that winter; but it is presumed the other still lingers in
his old haunts, waiting, perhaps, for he was an ardent
reformer, for the season of Austria's regeneration.

Amongst the mountains climbed here by Musafir was
the grey rock at the end of the second lake. So strictly
are the chamois preserved in these parts, that even entrance
into a certain range, of which this stone mountain is one,
is forbidden to the general traveller. Permission was never-
theless given to Musafir to explore it on condition he took
no gun with him, and made no attempt to molest the
beautiful chamois. Accordingly, in company with a Jäger,
one of the Emperor's keepers, he made the ascent. A
difficult and dangerous one it was, full of slippery places,
and headlong descents, but in the presence of the white
snow, outvying the rock itself in whiteness, and of the
distant chamois clearly visible, no sense of this was felt.
One chamois actually bounded to within fifty yards of the

travellers, and stood gazing at them from a point jutting out over a precipice. Suddenly he seemed aware of the dangerous proximity, for with a bound he sprang upwards, whilst the rattling of the stones below broke the silence of the scene.

The Jäger was a charming young fellow; he had served as a soldier in the Italian war, and gave vivid accounts of the mismanagement that had led to the disaster at Magenta. There, he said, the division with which he served, were thirty-six hours without food; in the presence of the enemy they received no orders at all; not a man was there in the force but believed that they had only to advance to be victorious, but for forty-eight hours there was no superior officer to give the order. Of Giulay and of Clam-Gallas he spoke with the most undisguised contempt.

The Emperor himself, though a strict preserver of game and very fond of killing chamois, is not considered by his subjects to be much of a sportsman. Instead of climbing the hills, in a true Jäger-like fashion,—the only satisfactory mode of placing oneself in competition with the chamois,— he has a sort of "machân" made for himself at the foot of the steep portion of the mountain. In this he sits, and waits for the game which Jägers and others drive towards him. It is an occupation scarcely worthy of a sportsman, even when that sportsman is an Emperor!

Our travellers quitted these lovely lakes and the good people of the Krähe with regret on the 12th June. The kind landlady's parting words were, "Send us some more English, we like to have the English"; and yet, this wish could scarcely have been expressed in the hope of making extraordinary profits out of that people; for, on examining his bill for eight days, Musafir found that the total, including board, lodging, beer, washing, scarcely exceeded three pounds. This was certainly not ruinous, yet it is probable that the Austrian lodgers paid even much less.*

Walking the five miles back to Ebensee, our travellers drove thence to Ischl. The day was bright and warm, and the view all the way lovely. The road lay along the banks of the swiftly-flowing Traun, with its clear, bright green waters, always charming. The beauty of the foliage, though not of the form of the hills, increased as they advanced. At length Ischl, and, in Ischl, the hotel Kaiserin Elisabeth,

---

* In 1871, Musafir revisited the Krähe. On entering the room he saw the good old landlady seated at her mid-day meal with her maidens. She looked at him, and then, without recognition, said, in the homely parlance of the Austrian peasantry, "Grüss Gott." Musafir then asked after the Krähmeyer. "He will be here soon," she replied, repeating the expression, "Grüss Gott." "Oh," said Musafir, "I see you don't know me." She looked at him attentively, walked straight up to him, seized both his hands, and then said with emphasis, "I do know you; you are the Herr who was with us in 1863-4. Ah!" she added, "we did not hear from you, and feared you must have been killed in one of those *Mexican* wars." The Krähmeyer shortly came in, looking as gay and sprightly as ever. The warmth of their reception could not have been exceeded.

In November 1871, the Krähmeyer had to quit his beautiful forest home. The Government officials had for years cast a longing eye upon it, and, fearing that on the death of the Krähmeyer it might revert to some relation, they persuaded him, rather authoritatively, to sell it to the Government, on condition of another house being built for him at Langbath. That house was erected on the Krähmeyer's own plans, and he and his family moved into it in December 1871. Musafir visited them there in 1878, and received as cordial a welcome as ever. The Krähmeyer still retains, for himself and friends, the right of fishing in the lakes.

kept by a most obliging host, Herr Endmoser, a Bavarian, were reached. Without being in any sense grand, Ischl is very beautiful. The five valleys which meet here cause such a variety of shape and size in the hills that different aspects are presented from every point of view. Coming from the more beautiful scenery of the Langbather lakes, this at Ischl was still pleasing, though from a different cause. It lacked the majestic grandeur and classic beauty of the first, but it had a soft and captivating air, as if inviting the traveller to stop and rest in its charms. The best view of Ischl itself is to be obtained from the new hotel,—the Actien Hotel. This hotel was designed by a very fine fellow named Bauer, formerly the proprietor of the Kaiserin Elisabeth; but the magnificent scale on which it was erected quite ruined him, and it now belongs to a company. Bauer was a model host, not grasping, but civil, obliging, and attentive, and, what is more, was beloved by the peasantry of the neighbouring villages and mountains. His taste is evinced by the selection of the ground for the hotel, the view from which is most pretty. The deep green verdure of the mountains is well set off by the light green of the Traun, which, running immediately under the windows of the Kaiserin Elisabeth Hotel, separates the town of Ischl from the suburbs on the right bank.

Ischl is famous for its salt-mines and its salt and mud baths, the two last being useful for chest affections. But it is more honoured now as the summer residence of the Austrian Court and the Austrian nobility. Here the Emperor has a beautiful estate, especially dear to the Empress, as on its ground she was betrothed. It abounds with villas constructed in the Swiss style, and boasts of a theatre, a concert-room, reading-rooms, and other places of amusement. Ischl is not indeed the sort of place which our travellers would have made their head-quarters. Not only is it too fashionable for those who do not come only to see and to be seen, but situated in a valley, its climate is somewhat relaxing. It wants, too, the boldness of scenery by which other places near it are distinguished. Still it is extremely pretty, and the excursions to be made from it are many and varied.

A general impression prevails that Ischl is a very dear place. That it is more expensive than the surrounding and neighbouring villages is true; and Englishmen unacquainted with Austrian ways may very often be imposed upon. The Musafirs, however, who stopped six days at the Kaiserin Elisabeth (then reputed the best and most expensive hotel at Ischl) found that their total hotel disbursements for that period amounted exactly to four guineas, everything included—no great outlay for the Biarritz of Austria!

Leaving Ischl on the 7th our travellers crossed the Traun, and drove in the direction of the lake of Grundl, the beauties of which had been reported marvellous. Their road lay through the little village of Lauffen, acquaintance with which, and with the good little landlady who kept the inn there, had been made by Musafir in some of his fishing excursions near Ischl. This lady was a young Viennese who had just married, and she and her husband had staked the first year of their married existence in the speculation of the little inn at Lauffen, it being her part to look after the guests at the inn, his after the excursionists on the river. Most admirably did they both perform their duties, and though the Musafirs left before the success of the speculation was decided, there could be little doubt but that her pleasing manners and excellent cuisine would entice a sufficient number of the idle residents of Ischl to trust themselves to her husband's strong arm on the Traun. Still she was anxious, and every wet day seemed to add to her anxiety, as Lauffen then had no visitors, and the length of the paying season was to that extent diminished.

Passing through Lauffen and the other villages on the Traun, the travellers came at length to the foot of the Pötschen-Joch, 3,224 feet high. Crossing this rather uninteresting height, they descended on the other side into a beautiful green valley, at the extreme end of which lay the village of Aussee, also on the Traun. Suddenly they came upon the view of the glorious Dachstein, 10,015 feet high, and of the splendid glacier, the Carl's Eisfeld, near its summit. This sea of pure snow, as it appeared, had, with the sun shining upon it, a most dazzling and beautiful effect. On the other side of the valley, contrasting with the Dachstein, is the Loser, 6,000 feet, of grey stone, whose castle-like turrets are very fine indeed, whilst the smiling green valley between caused both to stand out with the greater boldness. A drive of about three-quarters of an hour takes the traveller to the little town of Aussee, very picturesquely situated. Thence to the lake of Grundl is nearly three miles along the Traun, through an extremely pretty country. The Traun here runs like a torrent, looking gloriously. All at once a turn is reached, and the Grundl lake appears. Such

THE KELLNERIN.

a piece of water! Nearly five miles in length and upwards
of two in breadth; very deep evidently. On the northern
side of it a chain of high mountains, some of them covered
with snow, and all prettily wooded; on the southern side a
range of lesser height for the most part beautifully covered
with trees, lovely from their varying tints. On the further,
or eastern side, are bare rocks, rising almost perpendicularly
from the earth; at the foot of them a small village on the
green foreground. But what increased the charm of this
lake immensely, was the smiling green grass-land between
the mountains on the northern side and the lake. On this
were some pretty cottages which, with their inhabitants, gave
life and vividness to the scene. The first glimpse of this
spot was charming, and our travellers found that its enchant-
ment increased daily. Each passing hour brought to light
some new beauty, some till then undiscovered charm in this
most lovely place.

The little inn at which our travellers stopped is imme-
diately at the head of the lake, commanding nearly its entire
length, though a turn at the extreme end prevents it from
being seen. A more perfect sight for an inn it is difficult
to conceive. It is a three-storied house, prettily built, and
very well arranged.* In front of it, immediately on the
banks of the lake, is a little pavilion built in the Swiss
style, in which guests generally take their meals. It is a
place, too, in which one can sit, and read write or work,

---

* This inn was sold in 1867 to a Styrian gentleman, and converted
by him into a villa. There is, however, another most comfortable inn,
kept by Schramml, on the borders of the lake.

all day long. This inn was built some years ago by the Emperor's "Fischmeister," Kaim; a thoroughly honest, fine-hearted fellow. No man more keen than he to explore the lake with the Englishman in search of the finny tribe. He has had the honour of receiving the Emperor Francis, with whom he was a great favourite, within the walls of his house. But poor Kaim is now old and infirm, and is forced to lodge in the dwelling-place of which he was once sole master. It is now rented to a man named Grogger, who has another business in Aussee, leaving his wife to manage at Grundl. The wife is a very tidy, good-humoured, bustling housewife, and the best cook in Austria. Not even in Paris will the epicure be better treated than in the little inn, the Archduke John, on the banks of the lovely lake of Grundl. She possesses, too, the faculty of getting good servants. Of these there were only two at the little inn besides herself. One of them, Elise, was being trained up in cookery, occasionally waiting at the table. The other, Fanny, a modest, pretty brunette, was the kellnerin, or waitress, and a better, a more thoughtful, or more attentive handmaid, there never was in the world. It was a sight worth seeing, to watch these two girls, on the Sunday when the place was crowded, waiting on a dozen tables at once, never making a mistake, always ready at the right moment, and doing it with an aptitude, a grace, an exactness which claimed and always won admiration.

Another hanger-on of the little inn was a brother of old Fischmeister Kaim. He was a peasant in the neighbourhood, but during his brother's life-time had acted as admiral of the fleet of boats attached to the inn. This

was still in a measure his work. He had contracted the
nickname of the *Kanzler* or Chancellor,—not on account
of his aptitude at figures, for, poor fellow, he could neither
read nor write,—but it clung to him from the designation
of his cottage. He was the guide to all the beauties in
the neighbourhood; his the hand to propel the canoe, or
to assist in capturing the lake-trout. A hard-handed, good-
hearted, honest fellow was he,—may his life be prolonged.*

But the lake-beauties of this place were not limited
to the Grundl. Paddled by the Kanzler to the eastern
end,—a work with one man of about an hour and a
quarter,—the explorer disembarks near the village under
the bare rocks already alluded to, and walks under their
shadow till he comes to the Traun—here a narrow river
with clear water of a brownish hue;—ascending this he
enters a pretty wood, and in about a quarter of an hour
reaches the lake of Töplitz. This is a wonderful lake.
Grand in its solitude, surrounded by mountains covered for
the most part with the thickest foliage. Not a sound is
heard, save that made by the Traun as it leaves the deep
recesses of the lake, and by the little rills, which, gathering
as they descend, pour down the sides of the mountains
like torrents, and which keep up the store of water.
A stone on its banks marks the spot where the late Arch-
duke John—the defeated of Hohenlinden and once Regent
of Germany—wooed and won the fair daughter of the
innkeeper of Aussee. This lake is about half the length
of that of Grundl, and much less in breadth; in depth

---

* I saw him again in 1864 and 1871: he was drowned in 1876.

it far exceeds it, deep as that is. It is grand, solitary, and lovely. One returns from it, however, to the Grundl with a greater appreciation of the charms of that surpassing lake. It has the life, the variety, the cheerful gaiety in which this one is deficient. Before this return, however, a visit must be made to the Kammer lake. This is but five minutes' rather rough walking from the further end of the Töplitz lake, and it is well worth that trouble. Though very small the Kammer lake is extremely beautiful. Bare rocks rise to a height of about four thousand feet on its northern side, and contrast beautifully with the wooded hills opposite; whilst from a fissure, two-thirds of the height of the former, trickling down its face into the lake, may be seen a thin line of water,— the source of the beautiful Traun. It is quite a gem of its kind,— the solitude lending it a peculiar charm. The trip to and from the inn at the Grundl lake occupies from four to five hours. The old Kanzler enjoys the office of Cicerone, and never tires of pointing out the spot on the Töplitz lake, where he and an English gentleman and lady spent the entire night, the Englishman engaged in fishing, and having, it would appear, most wonderful sport.

Independently of the enjoyment to be had at the Grundl lake and its tributaries, in the way of fishing, boating, and climbing the beautiful mountains, full of chamois, by which it is surrounded, it is likewise a capital place from which to make excursions. Grogger, the landlord, has first-rate cattle in his stable, to be let out on reasonable terms; besides which, the walks are, some of them, most lovely. Amongst these may be noted the walk to Alt-

CATECHISMO
DE
AUSTRALIA

ALT-AUSSEE AND THE LOSER

Aussee, about five miles distant across the forest. Emerging from this, one comes into a series of green, undulating meads, with the glorious Dachstein in the distance. Alt-Aussee is a very pretty little village, boasting of a lake called the Au lake, and a very tidy little inn, where the stranger is carefully attended to. The cottages in this village, as in the neighbourhood of the Grundl lake, are clean and well kept, and our travellers remarked that there was not one which did not make itself attractive by the flowers in the window. The peasantry were well-to-do, hearty, cheering, and most civil and obliging. Another pretty walk is to the Netten, or Eden lake; a third, still prettier, across the mountains, to Obertraun. But, indeed, of pretty walks there is no end.

It is the custom in Austria to pasture the cows near the summits of the mountains. On the various alms, or pasturages, therefore, at various degrees of elevation there are built little huts or cottages called, in Switzerland, châlets, but in Austria, Almhütte. But there is a difference between the two;—that whereas in Switzerland the châlets are generally remarkable for their filth, and are kept by men who are always grasping and sometimes surly,—in Austria the Almhütte are models of cleanliness, and are kept by mountain-maidens, who are always clean and fresh-looking, often pretty, always unaffected and anxious to please. The first visit to one of these Almhütte was made by our travellers from the lake of Grundl. Piloted by the Kanzler, they set forth early one morning up the wooded sides of one of the mountains to the north of the lake. The ascent was stiff, but in an hour and a half the green patch of level ground was reached, and here were the Almhütte visible. They were so clean, and in such neat order; the butter, milk, and cream were laid so invitingly on the shelves, that, out of breath as they were, our travellers could not help expressing their admiration. Whilst last, not least, the aspect of the Sennerinnen—as the girls who follow this occupation are called in Austria—was so bright and pretty, they were so fresh-looking, so clean, so glad to welcome the Engländer,—that it was quite a fairy scene. They were prompt with their offers of fresh milk to the strangers, and one of them even set about preparing a cake, of the nature of those on which the mountaineers live, and very much resembling oatmeal porridge, with this exception that while it is being stirred up they put a lump of butter in the middle. Musafir tasted this and liked it, but his wife did not much fancy it. She made amends, however, by partaking of the beautifully fresh milk which the girls freely offered. Meanwhile the old Kanzler began to chaff them about the peasants who courted them, and about the dancing which took place on the green alm in front of the Almhütte. They laughingly denied, however, that they had any visitors beyond stray ones such as those who were then with them. By this time their simple meal was ready. After its conclusion, to amuse their guests, they began a charming Jodel, or mountain song. It is by these they recall their cows from the distant pastures in the evening, and it may well be surmised that never have these old mountains echoed back more pleasing harmony than that made by the voices of these Styrian maidens. On this occasion they continued their wild music long after their guests had left them, for the strain of it was heard after the Almhütte and its fair occupants were out of sight.

Of the boats under the charge of the Kanzler at the lake of Grundl, some are built on the model of the English wherry, others are simple canoes, not unlike the open dinghy of India, but there is a third kind peculiar to the place. This is a small flat-bottomed boat, with room in it but for one person. The sculler sits on the flat bottom, and takes in both hands a long propeller with blades at ends. This is dipped into the water alternately on either side, and by its means the boat is sent along at considerable speed. In managing a boat of this sort, the first difficulty for the sculler is to balance himself. This is at first by no means easy, as the little skiff is extremely light, and its rather high sides catch every breath of wind. This surmounted, the next object is to use the propeller, first, so as to avoid upsetting the skiff, and, secondly, to send it on at speed. It is astonishing to notice the dexterity attained by the Styrian peasants in this respect. There are, indeed, few prettier sights than that of a peasant girl in the becoming costume of the country, propelling one of these tiny boats, and endeavouring, by the exercise of greater skill, to avoid the pursuit which one of the opposite sex, relying on superior strength, would at once inaugurate. To watch how, going at a moderate pace, she would allow her enemy to come by rapid strokes nearly alongside, then, suddenly stopping, would see him forge far ahead, whilst she skilfully altered her course; to watch him coming on again more furiously, only to be again baffled by some other manœuvre, until she, the weaker, either returned unconquered, or, forcing him to confess his inferiority, paddled on in amity with her late opponent, was a sight that always interested the bystanders, and called forth excited remarks on the capabilities of the rival parties. It is one which to be appreciated should be seen.

Among the other residents at the little inn during the stay there of our travellers were a German lady and her daughter. Very pleasant, friendly people were they; the mother especially well-informed and clever. In their company many pleasant excursions were made. The daughter was a great swimmer. Almost every day about 11 o'clock she used to enter the wherry, and, pulling out about a mile, turn a corner, don her bathing-clothes, and take a header into the lake, leaving the boat to drift. She would, however, after a short swim, make for it, and getting over the side, would dress and pull again for the shore, looking far fresher and gayer than if she had adorned herself in her own room.

The only drawback to the pleasure of the sportsman at the Grundl lake arose from the absolute veto placed on fishing in its waters. It appeared that these lakes were under the superintendence of one of the Imperial rangers, a certain Herr Brandeis, and this man, for some reason of his own, had registered a vow that so long as the right lay in his gift, no Englishman should exercise it. This resolve of his was bitterly resented by Grogger and the innkeepers of Aussee, for it had the effect of driving Englishmen to other parts of the country, where the authorities were less churlishly disposed. But Brandeis was inexorable. The matter, however, has since been brought to the notice of the Austrian authorities, and an order has been issued

granting fish licences to all sportsmen, on the payment of a
florin per diem. This churlishness on the part of Brandeis
was the only piece of incivility experienced by our travellers
in Austria. To Musafir it was of little moment, as the
Grundl lake and its neighbourhood were too beautiful to
require any extra excitement ; but of all those who expressed
indignation, none came near the old Kanzler. "Fish without
leave," was his reiterated advice. To have followed it, how-
ever, would have been to break one of the soundest maxims
for all travellers,—never knowingly to infringe the laws of
the country in which they may find themselves.

At length it became necessary to quit even the beautiful
Grundl lake, and our travellers resolved to drive across the
mountains into Bavaria, to the far-famed König's See, stop-
ping by the way at the many places worthy of their inspection
en route. With this object they hired a carriage and pair
from Grogger, at the rate, all expenses told, of a pound
per diem, and on the 29th June paid farewell to all the kind
friends they had made at the Grundl. We use the word
"friends" designedly, for even in that short period, those
honest-hearted Styrians, whom they had never seen before,
had become so. Many were the wishes expressed for their
speedy return, for their safe journey, for another visit in next
year. At last they were off; their road taking them back
across the Pötschen Joch and as far as the village of
St. Agatha. Here they fell in with the road from Ischl, and
crossing the Traun, which is here very broad, they ascended
for two miles as far as the Gosau Mill. Here the carriage
was left, and the travellers proceeded in a boat to the little
village of Hallstadt, romantically situated on the lake of

that name. At Hallstadt they put up at a little inn called the Grüner Baum, where they found themselves most comfortable.

The lake of Hallstadt differs in every particular from that of Grundl. Neither so cheerful, nor so brightly beautiful, nor so taking, it has yet a distinct character of its own. Surrounded by very high mountains, so high that into one corner of the lake the sun never penetrates,—many of them splendidly wooded, some quite bare, but all lofty and striking, —the lake of Hallstadt possesses a grandeur approaching near to the melancholy. It is a place to see, but not to live at. Nevertheless it has its admirers; and one of its islands boasts even now of a little house erected on it by some holiday-making Etonians, and said to be by them periodically revisited. The little town is peculiar, being built up the sides of the hill; it has no roads, nor is there a horse in the place; all communication with the mainland is by water. The people looked sickly and deformed, caused partly probably by their having so little of the sun,—for the inhabitants of the village on the other side of the lake, the village of Obertraun, which is under a warm and sunny influence, are remarkable for their health and strength.

Near Hallstadt is a waterfall possessing some local renown. The walk to it, up a gorge between two mountains, is pretty and picturesque, but the fall itself is rather poor. It does not at least constitute the attraction that would draw visitors to Hallstadt. That attraction is to be found rather in the majestic grandeur of the mountains, and the sombre beauty of the lake.

The next day our travellers drove to Golling, the last con-

siderable Austrian town, on the direct road to the König's
See. The first part of the drive from Gosau Mill to Gosau is,
from many causes, extremely interesting. In the first place
it is very pretty; the two little lakes at Gosau vying with any
scenery in the world. To reach these, the traveller branches
off the direct road at Gosau, and drives through a clean but
scattered village to a very rude little inn, kept by the village
smith. It is advisable for the traveller to take his meal
under the trees outside the house, as this place is an
exception to the cleanliness for which Austria is otherwise
remarkable. The people, however, are simple and honest,
and will bring fresh milk and eggs, and will even make that
most delicious and easily prepared of all condiments—an
Austrian omelette. After the meal a guide makes his
appearance and takes the traveller to the first Gosau lake—
an extremely pretty walk of three-quarters of an hour. This
lake is small, but beautifully situated. Near it on one side,
rise up the Donner Kogeln, 6,732 feet high, whose dark grey
summits, shaped like thunder-bolts, seem as though they had
fallen from heaven; a little further, the Dachstein, seen here
to much greater advantage, and in far closer vicinity, than
at Aussee, shines resplendently; opposite these, beautiful
woods stretching back to a far distance from the lake.
There are no houses, no dwelling-places on the lake; a small
boat-house and a little canoe are the only signs that it is
sometimes visited. But this view, beautiful as it is, is as
nothing compared to those to be enjoyed during the walk to
the further lake. This takes the traveller through a most
lovely forest, impervious to crinolines, with occasional rather
rough ascents. Ever and anon, however, the forest seems

as if by enchantment, to move aside his leafy screen, in order to disclose views of the most enchanting and bewitching beauty. In the first place the traveller sees, rising almost from its base, the magnificent Donner Kogeln, which, though not of the Dolomite order, possesses some of the peculiarities by which those mountains are distinguished; he has glimpses, marvellous in their beauty, of the Dachstein, until, reaching the second lake, he enjoys a full view of that glorious mountain, as it rises by successive spurs from its further bank. Then again, the varied foliage contrasts strikingly with the dazzling snow, whilst the bare rocks of dark grey, and others covered here and there with moss and verdure, come to add to the glories of the walk. It is indeed an excursion that, once undertaken, is never to be forgotten.

The other reason which makes a visit to Gosau interesting is, that it constitutes a small Protestant family in the midst of an overgrown Catholic community. In the early part of the eighteenth century, the fathers of the present occupants of the little valley found in it a refuge from the tyranny of the Archbishops of Salzburg. There, in spite of much persecution, and repeated attempts at conversion, have they since remained, firm in their faith. To that Protestant faith they still continue devoted, nor in this instance has persistent constancy been without reward. For now, to the number of 1,300, they are unmolested on account of their opinions, and possess even a church and pastors of their own.

Returning thence, the carriage is once more gained, and the Tännen Gebirge, a range whose precipitous sides attract admiration, is passed on the road to Abtenau. Not stopping to examine the wonderful cavern, discovered in that range, known as Frauenloch, our travellers press on. At Abtenau, a simple village, boasting two fair inns, the traveller sleeps, or, if he be adventurous, pushes three hours further on to Golling. Our travellers pursued the latter course, being anxious to see Pass Lueg and the famous waterfall of the Schwarzbach.

Waterfalls are not in general worth the trouble of going very far to see, but this of Golling is an exception to the rule. It descends about three hundred feet down a nearly perpendicular rock, and is voluminous and grand, seen from almost any point. But let the traveller ascend, as he can easily by steps artificially formed, to the very summit of the fall, and he sees that which surprises him. He sees the water, which is to constitute the fall, issuing through a wide orifice out of the very centre of the mountain, as though it were flowing under a bridge or tunnel; it then collects in a natural reservoir, and empties itself over the rocks into the stream below. Now the question first arises: Whence does this water come? The natural answer is: From an imprisoned lake within the mountains. Indeed, the people of Golling assert this to be a fact that admits of no dispute, inasmuch as the lake has been navigated for about a hundred yards inside. The next question that suggests itself is this: Whence is this lake supplied with water? It is incessantly pouring water over the rocks, whence comes the fresh supply? It is popularly believed that it is fed by the König's See on the other side of the mountain, and lying at an elevation of eight hundred feet higher than that of the imprisoned lake. This may well be the case, but it has never positively been proved. Anyhow, the circumstance of a lake being imprisoned within a mountain is curious, and invites thoughts as to the unexplored wonders of nature, and of man's ignorance regarding them.

Pass Lueg was not on this occasion visited by our travellers, though the succeeding year Musafir atoned for this neglect. The next day they crossed the Austrian frontier near Hallein, and entered the Bavarian mountains.

At this point we break off from the unpublished journal. Not indeed because it is exhausted, for the Musafirs found Bavaria and Switzerland not less attractive than Austria. To continue, however, would cause us to exceed the allotted limits. Enough, we would fain hope, has been extracted to justify the assertion in which we indulged at the outset, that in a journey from India to Europe, the Anglo-Indian will find more than a recompense for many years of exile and toil. It is, indeed, our conscientious conviction that no man so much as the Anglo-Indian—if not corrupted by the over-accumulation of wealth, or spoilt and enervated by official position—would enjoy a journey of this nature. To him all is so new, so utterly unlike the routine of the life he has been accustomed to; there is so much variety, not only in the scenery of the country, but in the manners of the people, that whilst his faculty of enjoyment is greatly gratified, his mind opens itself to new views, to enlarged ideas, to instruction of which he has had but little knowledge. Few will deny that the tendency of a life-experience, or even of many years' experience, in one particular profession, in a daily recurrence of similar scenes, is to dwarf the mind and to

narrow the intellect. The knowledge that is gained in
that particular groove, of itself doubtless valuable, has even
sometimes the effect of unduly exalting that baser sort
of pride, which is indwelling in some minds. Because one
branch of a profession has been mastered, everything else
comes to be despised ; other men, who may not belong
to that profession, are thought to know nothing. It is as
an antidote to a poison of this sort that travelling is so
desirable. The men who hold such sentiments often require
nothing more than the opportunity of opening the eyes of
their minds, of seeing that these local questions, all-engross-
ing as they appear, are after all but local ; that they are
but infinitesimal parts of a greater whole ; that though the
mastery of them may stimulate the pride of a man, yet to
be entirely immersed in them lowers his intellectual capa-
bilities, and leaves him powerless to enjoy much that is,
in the highest sense of the word, enjoyable. It is impos-
sible to describe the buoyancy of spirits, the elasticity of
temperament, experienced by an Anglo-Indian who tries this
course for the first time. How magically do the wretched
local squabbles he has left behind him disappear from his
imagination ; how paltry and ridiculous they seem, should
a letter from India or any chance circumstance recall them !
How he laughs when he thinks of the lofty airs of local
dignitaries, of the tinsel decorations and assumed importance
of some of his Indian associates ! In a great part of
Europe at all events he finds beautiful nature, unaffected
manners, and the refined courtesy which is their certain
accompaniment. He sees that there prevails at the basis
of society a system of equality, tempered not by the

official position of the individual, but by intellect and acquirements. He finds out very soon that the stilted airs of officialism are only an impediment to real enjoyment. As these new ideas steal upon him by degrees, he feels accompanying them that buoyancy of heart and elasticity of spirit of which we have spoken, and he experiences an enjoyment long unfelt—the enjoyment of the beauties of a nature as yet free and unspoilt, and of a society unfettered by social restrictions or by artificial restraints.

It has been with the view to place a picture of this nature before our Anglo-Indian readers, that we have drawn so largely on the unpublished journal of Captain Musafir. There are, it is true, other routes than those which he followed, more enticing to the pedestrian and the sportsman. That which we have described is only one amongst many of those accessible to ladies; but the account of it will show that there is much that is worthy of being visited, something even that might be imitated, in the little-explored regions of much-abused Austria.

THE FIRST GOKAU LAKE.

II.

We left our friends the Musafirs at Golling, the last town of any note in the direct route between Hallstadt and the König's See. This direct route consists, however, but of a pathway across the mountains, involving an ascent of nearly 6,000 feet and a walk of seven hours. This walk is justly celebrated; inasmuch as from the summit of the Königsberg-Alp there is a most lovely view of the König's See, with the snow-capped Watzmann rising in all its glorious majesty from its very surface, the Untersberg frowning in the distance. In the descent there is much that is picturesque and beautiful, not to speak of a fine waterfall. But to enjoy this walk fine weather is absolutely necessary, and as this condition was wanting on the occasion we are referring to, the rain falling in torrents and showing no symptoms of cessation, the Musafirs determined not to attempt it. The same reason deterred them from trying the alternative mountain route across the Rossfeld Alp, a height of about 5,000 feet, a charming walk of about six hours. They were driven, therefore, to the choice of the third and least interesting route to Hallein by the road, thence across the Dürnberg, but little over two thousand feet high, to Berchtesgaden. The drive to Hallein was not very interesting, but it lasted only an hour. The town itself is famous for its salt-mines, which penetrate deeply into the Dürnberg; but after the natural wonders of Adelsberg, our travellers did not care to inspect the artificial caverns of Hallein, but pushed at once across the mountain. The ascent from Hallein is extremely steep, but, once on the top of the plateau, there is a continual though gradual descent towards Berchtesgaden. About half an hour after leaving Hallein our travellers crossed the Bavarian frontier, the only perceptible difference being that, whereas in Austria the subordinate officials wore a uniform of black and yellow, in Bavaria they donned a light blue and white.

From the Bavarian frontier to Berchtesgaden is a drive of about an hour, over a pretty undulating country, surrounded by lofty mountains, conspicuous amongst which is the Watzmann, 8,578 feet high, and covered with eternal snow. The shapes of all the mountains in this part of the country are very grand and picturesque, and the beauty of the scene is greatly heightened by their many points of difference from one another. The town of Berchtesgaden, which our travellers were now approaching, is one of the prettiest in Germany, being situated on an undulating plateau, green, smiling, and very cheerful, on the banks of the little river Albe, which runs out of the König's See, three miles south of the town. Seen from a height, this cheerful town, with its pretty wooded foreground, and the mountains towering behind it, forms a picture which none who have seen it will easily forget, which remains imprinted for ever on the memory of those between whom and it exists the all but impassable barrier of six thousand miles of black water.

It formed, however, no part of the intentions of the Musafirs to stop at Berchtesgaden, beautiful as it is. When at Ischl they had formed the acquaintance of an English gentleman and his wife, who had spent the previous autumn and part of the winter in the vicinity of Berchtesgaden, and who had indicated to them a place far better suited to their purposes than any of the inns, none of them then very good, of that town. This place was a small country inn in the little village of Unterstein, about two miles nearer the König's See, kept by a land-lady who had herself written a cookery book, and who also possessed the faculty of making her guests feel, whilst in her house, as if they were in their own home. It is necessary, as we shall be in his company for a few days, to give some short account of the English gentleman who had pointed out this resting-place to our travellers. We will call him, as he calls himself, Wild Hunter. He was, as his name signifies, an inveterate sportsman, and, though a barrister by profession, he had abandoned the glories of the circuit and the witticisms of the robing-room, to indulge in his favourite pursuit of seeking the feathered and finny tribe all over Europe. He had ransacked Brittany, had exhausted Austria, and was now directing all his energies against the rivers of Bavaria. And not alone against her rivers. We have said that he had passed the previous autumn and part of the winter in the neighbourhood of Berchtesgaden, but we have not yet mentioned the purpose. That will show, more than anything, the absolute devotion of Wild Hunter to sport. It happens that between the countries of Austria and Bavaria, is a mountain called the Untersberg, about 6,000 feet high. This mountain, thus situated between the two countries, forms a kind of debateable land, to which the Austrian and Bavarian sportsmen think they have each equal right. The consequence is that, whilst on every other mountain the game is carefully preserved, in this it is hunted by all classes, with the result that not only have the animals hunted become few in number, but those that remain are so wild as scarcely to be approached. Their numbers, however, have been accurately ascertained by the sportsmen of the neighbourhood, and in the winter of the year of which we are writing it was known that nine chamois yet remained on the mountain. To get a shot at one of these nine was at that time the great object of Wild Hunter's ambition. To this end he located himself and his wife in a little inn at the foot of the mountain, and seized every opportunity of ascending it for the purpose we have indicated. He made friends with the Royal Jägers, and in their company planned frequent campaigns against the chamois. The Untersberg is in many places a difficult, and in some even a dangerous mountain. But neither difficulty nor danger daunted Wild Hunter. After a little practice he was able to climb the most rocky and precipitous ascents, and to follow wherever the sons of the mountain would lead. But all his exertions were vain. He never, we believe, once approached within shooting distance of a chamois. Rendered wary by frequent pursuit, these agile animals always managed to anticipate their pursuer, and the sight of one of them bounding across a distant chasm was the sole return received by Wild Hunter for his all but solitary life and his repeated toils. A chance was, however, afforded him, as we shall have occasion to show, of attaining the object of his ambition before finally taking leave of Bavaria.

Wild Hunter had spent the remainder of the winter, the spring, and part of the summer, elsewhere, but he had returned to the little inn near the König's See to indulge in the excellent trout-fishing in the Albe, and he and his wife had arranged to meet the Musafirs at that place, to enjoy together the beauties of the surrounding scenery, and a few casts in the tempting waters. That is the reason why the Musafirs drove through, instead of stopping at, Berchtesgaden, and put up at the little house in the village of Unterstein, kept by the authoress of the cookery book.

Though not striking in outside appearance, the place was within a model of everything that was clean and comfortable. There were no other guests but the Wild Hunters, so it was to all intents a private dwelling-place. Its situation was very pretty. Underneath the Watzmann, in a smiling valley, full of orchards and gardens, two minutes' walk from the river, and but fifteen from the König's See, it was a site for a king. Indeed, so much had it been appreciated, that close to it, Count Arco,* the most famous sportsman in Bavaria, and, perhaps, in Germany, had built a country seat, adorned with the many products of his never-failing

---

* The name of this nobleman is familiar to everyone in Southern Germany. One of his feats, the climbing up a mountain-rock to capture a young eagle in its nest after having shot the old birds, on ladders which, when tied together, did not reach up to the nest—a task which the boldest Jägers had declined,—has formed the text of a ballad known all over Bavaria.

rifle. The little inn was just as favourably situated as the seat, and our travellers found here, as in Austria, that kindness and consideration have taken strong root in the nature of the German housewife.

It was, as we have said, within fifteen minutes' walk of the König's See, of all the lakes in Germany the most famous, and challenging comparison in some respects with the glories of Switzerland and North Italy. More grand even than the lake of Hallstadt and much more bright and sunny, possessing much of the wild beauty of the gems of Langbath, and of the little lake of Töplitz, yielding only in soft and enchanting beauty to the Grundl-See, it is yet more striking even than that. Imagine a piece of water, a rich blue in colour, and clear beyond comparison, very deep, surrounded by lofty mountains rising perpendicularly from its surface to a height of upwards of 8,000 feet, some of them bare rock, so smooth, and rising so directly, that a boat's crew touching at that point would have no means of landing, some of them covered with rich and picturesque foliage. Round the lake is no pathway, no means to make a circuit on foot; one must traverse its surface to see all its glories. More known and more renowned than any of the other German lakes we have referred to, it is much more visited by the tourists; and the firing of guns made by members of this class to cause an echo, is apt, perhaps, to interrupt the intense feeling with which the lover of nature gazes on it for the first time. It is not very large; in length it extends about six miles, and its average breadth is perhaps a mile and a half; yet it is so winding that the end is not seen from the embarking place, and it has

this advantage, that each turn brings some new beauty
into view. About two-thirds of the distance from the
starting point a little island, called St. Bartholomew, is
reached, famous for the charr and lake-trout, which, caught
in the lake, are preserved here in ponds for the consumption
of the traveller. On this little island is the king's hunting-
box, but the Jäger in charge of it acts also the part of host,
and an excellent thing he makes of it. On the walls of
the entrance room of the little inn are pictures of lake-trout
and charr of enormous size, some of them about sixty pounds,
which from time to time have been taken from the deep
waters of the lake. Another picture represents a bear
attacking a boat as it is crossing the lake in the middle
of winter. This is interesting inasmuch as it is the true
representation of an actual fact, and as the bear in question
—which was then killed—was the last of its species seen
in the mountains round the König's See. This event
occurred, if Musafir was correctly informed, some forty
years ago. To see the island of St. Bartholomew and the
mountains behind it in their greatest perfection, the traveller
should land at a point on the opposite side of the lake
called the Wallner island. The view from this is glorious.
There is the little island of St. Bartholomew in the fore-
ground, and the splendid Watzmann with his rugged wall
of rock rising up to an unseen height behind it. It is
difficult to decide whether it is most attractive in fine bright
sunshine, or when the mountains and foliage are under
the alternate influence of cloud and sun. The varying
tints caused by the latter, the dark angry appearance of
the Watzmann suffering under the frowns of Heaven, are

perhaps more striking, though infinitely less cheerful, than when the sun pours forth its mightiest power on its double head of snow. Beyond the König's See at a distance of about a quarter of a mile, is another though a much smaller lake called the Ober-See, which partakes of the grandeur and wild picturesqueness of its companion.

But not alone the lakes of this lovely district challenge admiration. In every direction its mountains invite visits from the lovers of nature. On the Eastern side of the lake from the Wallner island, there is a most glorious walk to the Gotzen Alp, an ascent of about three hours. The view from the summit of this is very fine, and not only that, but during the ascent the traveller is compelled many and many a time to linger, and even to stand motionless, in order to gaze at the ever-changing scenery offering itself to his view. Then again, the walk from the Gotzen Alp to the Salet Alp invites the adventurous traveller to scramble through the royal preserves, abounding in deer and chamois, to the crest of the Landthalwand; thence by narrow paths to the Fischunkl Alp. The Watzmann, the Göll, the Grünsee Tauern, the Viehkogel, and the Funtensee Tauern, are likewise well worthy of being attempted. The last-named, from its summit (8,393 feet), commands a splendid view of those giants of the Central Alps, the Venediger and the Gross Glockner. But it would take up too much space to describe all the excursions, —some of them more distant—to make which the little hostelry at Unterstein formed excellent head-quarters. One of these, across the mountains to Reichenhall, is known and appreciated by every traveller. Ramsau, and the little lake some two miles beyond it, the Hinter See, the delight of the painter, constitute an extremely pretty drive. The scenery at the Hinter See is so different from the scenery on the other parts of the district ; there is more foreground, the mountains are not so near, and yet there are some in the vicinity, the Steinberg, the Mühlsturzhorn, the Hochkalter, and the Edelweisslahnerkopf, most picturesque in form, and all well repaying an ascent.

It was in the midst of this scenery, sometimes on the bosom of the König's See, now making an excursion to a distant mountain, now to an enticing lake, ever enjoying the glorious mountain air, and the bright sunniness of smiling Bavaria, that the Musafirs in the society of their friends spent some ten or twelve days of their holiday. Nor was fishing entirely neglected. The very first morning after their arrival at the little inn, Musafir was fortunate enough to capture, with very light tackle and a fly, a trout upwards of two pounds and a half in weight, and which was destined the next day to contribute to the table of the ex-king Louis, who arrived that morning at Berchtesgaden. As reference has been made to fishing, it may be as well to point out the method necessary to be adopted by an Englishman fond of the sport, and who may be desirous of enjoying it. The rivers are all rented to individuals, most of them inn-keepers. These have the exclusive right to all the fish in the water they rent, and no one else can try for them without their permission. Now trout and grayling are looked upon, both in Austria and Bavaria, as very great delicacies, and they command a proportionate price. The plan, therefore, adopted by the inn-keepers is to have attached to their hotels two or three tanks kept filled by a constant supply of running

9

water. Into these tanks all the fish caught in the river are thrown, and kept till required for the use of the passing guest. Under these circumstances it becomes an object to each inn-keeper to have a fresh supply of trout and grayling constantly brought in from the river. Hence they, in general, scruple not to give free permission to the Englishman to fish, provided he engage to bring home alive all that he may catch. Means and appliances to this are not wanting. It becomes only necessary for the fisherman to hire a man, at the rate of about eighteen-pence a day, to accompany him. This man carries on his back a sort of barrel, with a small opening on the upper side and air-holes. Into this barrel all the fish caught are placed, and it is the business of the man to see that they are supplied with water, and that this water is constantly changed. In this way the engagement entered into with the landlord is easily kept. The system has this advantage, that the sportsman is under no obligation to anyone, for, if he be anything of a fisherman, his indulgence in sport is a great benefit to his host. Indeed, Musafir records that at one place where he stopped, the landlord offered to put him up for the entire season, and give him the best of the house for nothing, provided only he would keep the kitchen well supplied with the produce of his rod. But this was in an out-of-the-way place, in which no fish-tanks had been introduced.

But to return. It had been agreed upon between Musafir and Wild Hunter, that whilst the ladies were enjoying a rest after a trip made to Ramsau and the Hinter See, they would ascend the Untersberg, sleep in an Alm-hütte on its summit, and either in the cool of the evening, or in the early grey of

the morning, make an attempt on the roebuck, of which there
were a few. In pursuance of this resolve they left the little
inn at mid-day, and walked eight miles to the village of
Schellenberg, just under the Untersberg. Here they dined,
and here they were joined by a Bavarian Jäger, who had
accompanied Wild Hunter in many of his excursions to the
same mountain the previous autumn. At 5 p.m., they started
to ascend the mountain. To do this they had to climb first
a smaller range called the Ettenberg, extremely well-wooded,
and considered the most likely place for roebuck, then to
descend a little till a junction was formed with the Untersberg. The ascent of the Ettenberg took about an hour; but
not a roebuck was seen; then, after descending, the three
commenced the more difficult task of the Untersberg. After
an hour and a half's hard work of constant ascent, the Jäger
called a halt, as this was also considered a good place for
roedeer. But after beating about for half an hour no sign of
them appeared, and the ascent was continued. From this
place to the Alm-hütte was an hour's stiff pull: indeed, some
parts of the ascent were very trying indeed. At length the
Alm-hütte was reached. Arrived there, the Jäger at once
knocked at the door, but, receiving no answer after repeated
knockings, he came to the conclusion that it had been left by
those in charge of it, and that the ascent to a hut further off
would have to be resumed. Fortunately, however, his last
knock met with a response, and it appeared that the old
couple who pastured the cows were not absent but asleep.
The three travellers at once groped their way through the
cow-sheds, and found themselves in a little room in which
were an old man just out of bed, and an old lady in the act of

getting out. These did not at all feel the gravity of the situation, but, giving our travellers a hearty welcome, they briskly began to light the fire, to bring seats, and to dry their wet clothes. They then went into an adjoining room, and brought out a bowl or two of the richest and most refreshing milk. Then kneeling before the fire, they set themselves to work to make some *schmarren* or porridge, the composition of which has been described in our first part. Of this Musafir and the Jäger partook heartily, but Wild Hunter did not much relish it. He, meanwhile, had recognised in the old couple acquaintances of the previous year, under whose slender roof he had often enjoyed a night's lodging on the mountains. It is difficult to describe their pleasure at seeing him again; their welcome was most hearty, and showed how much these simple people value those strangers, who do not consider it as derogating from their own importance to regard and treat them as men formed of the same clay, and shaped in the same mould. The conversation soon became general; the narrow escapes, the wildness of the chamois, the exploits of the poachers, the relative merits of the Austrian and Bavarian climbers, were topics which came easily to the surface, and were discussed with interest by all. At length it was time to turn in, and the three travellers were shown into a loft piled up with fresh hay. Taking off their shoes, they threw themselves on this, and slept soundly and comfortably till the small hours of the following day.

As they still hoped to get sight of a roebuck, the travellers were roused at half-past two in the morning. Putting on their shoes they went outside, had a good wash at a pump that was found there, drank a good draught of the delicious

STYRIAN JÄGER.

milk that was offered them, gave some small remuneration to their kind hosts, and started off. Their way lay for some time along the side of the mountain, alternately ascending and descending. After walking about three-quarters of an hour, they came upon another Alm-hütte; immediately after leaving which they found themselves amongst the *latschen* or brushwood, so useful to the climber. They still walked carelessly on, rather ascending, when suddenly the Jäger, who was in front, stopped, and put his hand up to his ear. A second later, he turned with a joyful glance to his companions, and whispering the word *Gemse* (chamois), made a sign to them to stoop down. He had heard, in fact, the peculiar sound made by the buck chamois in the ravine near to which they were walking. Immediately afterwards they caught sight of the animal going slowly down the ravine in front of them. At this sight, the Jäger gave his rifle to Musafir, and, whispering "Come quickly," bounded like a deer up the steep sides of a rock commanding the ravine. In a few seconds, Musafir was beside him, Wild Hunter halting within twenty yards. All knelt. The chamois was within sight, slowly moving towards the rock, at a distance of about a hundred yards. Suddenly he stopped. "Fire," whispered the Jäger to Musafir, whose rifle was directed at the animal. Musafir pulled the trigger, but, by a piece of almost unexampled ill-luck, the cap snapped. The rifle belonged to the Jäger, and it had been probably kept loaded for some days. Still the animal moved not. It was a beautiful sight to watch him with his head up in the air, as though distrustful, as though he had some warning of approaching danger. All this time Wild Hunter was taking a deliberate aim. It was curious that he who had toiled in this very mountain all the previous autumn and part of the winter, should thus have a chance offered him when least expected. At last he fired; the surrounding rocks re-echoed the sound. For a moment the chamois moved not, and then only slowly and hesitatingly, so much so that Wild Hunter, who believed he had hit him, made sure he must be wounded. For a few minutes the Jäger thought so too, and put on his dog. But some seconds after, the animal was seen bounding up the sides of the mountain, an almost certain indication that he was unhurt.

This adventure, exciting of its kind, served as a subject of discussion for the rest of their walk. The most cast down was the poor Jäger, who never ceased to lament over the misfortune of the cap. It so happened that this Jäger, though most daring and adventurous, was noted for his ill-luck. Something always happened at the critical moment to interfere with his success. He could not but be mortified, then, that such a slight mischance should have prevented the accomplishment of a feat, which, easy on many mountains, assumes on the Untersberg a more than ordinarily difficult character. Nor did he recover from his dejection all the morning.

The descent from the rock which our travellers had climbed to have a shot at the chamois was more difficult than they imagined. In the time of excitement men will go anywhere; but the cause of the excitement once passed, they often look at objects in a much more matter-of-fact light. Thus it was on the occasion of which we are writing. The descent chosen by the Jäger was not, perhaps, dangerous to life, but, being down smooth ledges of rock, with no grateful *latschen* to clutch hold of, it was certainly very threatening to limb. To men unpractised in mountaineering, indeed, long and deep descents are much more fatiguing and wearisome than ascents of the same character. That this preference for ascents is due solely to inexperience, or to want of skill in the use of the Alpine stock, is clear from the fact that, aided by this charmed supporter, the Jägers bound down very difficult places with apparent ease.

Our travellers, pursuing a slower pace, continued their steady descent till about 8 A.M., when they reached the village of Schellenberg, just in time to drink a cup of coffee before the *Eilwagen* (stage-coach) came up to give them a lift as far as Berchtesgaden. Thence they walked to the little inn, on arriving at which, a dip in the clear waters of the Albe gave them renewed life.

It is scarcely necessary to enter further into the details of their life and residence at this very pretty spot. One entire day—and a most delightful one—was spent on the König's See itself, others in rambles over the country, or in the excursions we have indicated. At length the Musafirs determined to move on towards Munich, taking on their way the splendid Austrian town of Salzburg, and the retired Bavarian village of Traunstein. They bade adieu then to Wild Hunter and his wife, leaving them both under the care of the kind lady of their little inn, and him with the conviction that he would yet capture more of the finny inhabitants of the Albe, and with the determination not to allow another winter to pass by without possessing the long-coveted trophy, which those who have shot a chamois have alone the right to wear.*

The distance from the little village of Unterstein to the town of Salzburg is about seventeen miles, the road interesting all the way, and the view approaching Salzburg extremely grand and picturesque. Salzburg itself is one of the most striking towns in Europe. In its centre rises a hill called the Mönchsberg, on the top of one of the spurs of which is a magnificent castle, formerly the residence of the Prince-Archbishops of Salzburg, but now dismantled. This castle is built in the old style, and gives to the town itself a most romantic appearance. Seen, indeed, from any approach, this picturesque building, loftily perched on a hill, beautifully wooded, and rising apparently from the very centre of the town, cannot fail to arrest the attention and to charm the eye. Between this hill and the river Salzach, dark, muddy, and swiftly flowing, are the principal streets of the town; on the other side of the river a companion hill to the Mönchsberg, the Capuzinerberg, rises to a height of 640 feet over the Salzach, and commands a most glorious view of the town and castle, with the dark Untersberg in the background, and the shining Watzmann in the distance. The summit of this hill, on which, by the way, is a very good little *auberge*, commands perhaps the best view of Salzburg itself, and

---

* This is the hair on the back of the chamois, which, formed into a sort of tuft, is worn in their hats by all Austrians and Bavarians who have shot a chamois. We may here add that late in that autumn, Wild Hunter succeeded in shooting a chamois at Garmisch in Bavaria,

STYRIAN PEASANT WOMAN.

of the mountains surrounding it.* It is one of those views which, once seen, engraves itself for ever on the memory.

The best hotel in Salzburg in those days was the Drei Alliirten, kept by a Mr. Jung, a most attentive and excellent host. He speaks English, attends to his business himself, and will always go out of his way to oblige his guests. Do they want to do some sight-seeing, to visit Berchtesgaden and the König's See, to make preparations for a walking tour, to change English or Bavarian money into Austrian, even to start on a fishing excursion, they have only to mention their wishes to Jung, and leave the rest to him. He will make every arrangement, and, what is often of no small importance and very rare, he will charge most moderately. Jung is not only civil and obliging himself, but he makes all his waiters the same. He keeps a capital cook, and his is the only hotel in Salzburg which is supplied with the famous *Kaltenhausen* ale, second to none in the world. Here also the traveller gets in perfection the red and white Vöslauer. The sparkling wine of that name is a fair substitute for champagne and costs but one-half. In a word, our travellers found at the Drei Alliirten all the attention of the smaller inns they had visited, combined with the luxuries incidental to a first-class town hotel.†

---

* One of the best descriptions of Salzburg and of the pretty places in its vicinity, such as Aigen, the Gaisberg, and Hellbrunn, is to be found in Baroness Tautphœus' novel of "Cyrilla."

† Should anyone be tempted by this description to place himself under the care of Mr. Jung, we deem it right to inform him that since the Musafirs visited Salzburg, he has given up the Drei Alliirten, and built a magnificent hotel of his own, near the railway terminus, called Hotel de l'Europe.

Our travellers stayed three days at Salzburg, making excursions to the various places of interest in the neighbourhood, and then started by rail to Traunstein, a little village across the Bavarian frontier, on the white Traun, of the fishing capabilities of which they had received marvellous accounts. In the same carriage with them there travelled a Prussian, a native of Berlin, who lost no opportunity of hinting the low estimation in which he held everything Austrian, and the infinite and overwhelming superiority of Prussia and the Prussians. He declared that with two shillings he could buy more in Berlin than with three gulden (six shillings) in Salzburg. A Bavarian in the carriage supported him in his hits against Austria; but when he too observed that they managed things differently in Bavaria, the Prussian quietly shrugged his shoulders, and made a grimace intimating, more plainly than words could convey, that he held Bavaria in much the same esteem as Austria. He continued to hint this in various ways during the journey.

Traunstein, to which the train in about an hour's time brought the Musafirs, is a pretty and very clean village on the white Traun; it is surrounded by hills, none of them, however, very near, but looking grand in the distance. The country about is pretty and well wooded, and the place being famed for the salubrity of its climate, is resorted to in considerable numbers by the Bavarians. It has several excellent inns, and these, during the summer and autumn, are well filled. The charges in all are extremely moderate. The Musafirs put up in that to which they had been recommended, the *Hirsch*, and found themselves there most comfortable. Amongst other places of amusement, Traunstein, like all German towns at all frequented during the summer, boasts of a small theatre, to attend which it is not necessary to don evening dress. The performances begin about seven o'clock and are over by ten, a far more rational procedure than in the great cities of Europe. Here, as at Gratz, at Lintz, and other places in Southern Germany, ices are brought in during the intervals between the acts, and are freely partaken of.

In this little town our travellers remained six days, Musafir having capital sport in the way of fishing. It was generally arranged that he and his wife should go out for the day, making for a spot fixed upon near the banks of the river, at once pretty and commodious. This became the head-quarters for the day. Musafir then fished the river for an hour or two, his wife either sketching or picking the ferns and wild flowers with which the place abounded. After the box, carried by the attendant porter, had been pretty well filled,—and all fish under half a pound in weight were returned to the river,—they sauntered home by a fresh path, or wandered in search of other beauties of nature.

One day an excursion was made to the Chiem-See, the largest lake in Bavaria. Starting early in the morning, they drove ten miles to Seebruck at the head of the lake, and whence they commanded a good view of a great part of it. It is an enormous piece of water, quite open, presenting a grand appearance from its mere size. Contrasted with the deep blue water of the König's See, the water of this lake is discoloured and dirty, and altogether it is not to be mentioned in the same list. Nevertheless it is far from being ugly. The hills on its southern and eastern sides are picturesque and well wooded. Two pretty islands, Frauenwörth and Herrenwörth deserve a visit, especially the first. It must nevertheless be admitted that to the traveller coming from the Austrian lakes and the König's See the effect of this lake is disappointing. He misses the points which make those lakes so enchanting—the overhanging mountains, the smiling foregrounds, the varying tints, the deep, clear, water. The Chiem-See more resembles an inland sea than one of the gems which add so much to the beauty of mountain scenery.

Two days later the Musafirs went on by rail to Munich, and stayed there nearly a fortnight. We do not propose to follow them in their inspection of the many points of interest in a city so well known and so much visited. The famous guide books of Murray and Baedeker are open to everyone, and point out clearly all that is worthy of inspection. The Musafirs, however, had always intended that Munich should form a point whence to plan fresh mountain excursions. It had been their idea to proceed in the direction of Innsbruck, taking on the way the beautiful lakes, Ammer See and Wurm See, then stopping at Ober Ammergau, the scene of the events described in Baroness Tautphœus' novel of "Quits," thence by the Walchen and Achen lakes to Zell in Zillerthal, and from that place to Innsbruck. It would have been a charming trip, and Musafir was divided between that and Switzerland, when a letter from a friend decided him in favour of the latter.

This friend was a young Anglo-Indian, whom we will call Punjaubee, who had lately married, and who was then on his way with his bride to Lucerne with the intention of making thence, with her and some of the members of her family, excursions into the best-appreciated parts of the country in the neighbourhood. Both Musafir and his wife jumped at the idea of a tour in such company, and the order of the day was therefore passed for Lucerne.

The direct route by the railway from Munich towards Lucerne takes the traveller to the ancient city of Augsburg, thence to Lake Constance, which is traversed from its eastern point at Lindau to its western at Schaffhausen, whence the railway takes him direct to Lucerne. The Musafirs could not pass so famous a city as Augsburg without paying it a visit, and the day they spent in it more than repaid them for the delay. It was interesting to notice that part of the town, which was still a flourishing city in the time of the glories of the old Roman Empire; to examine buildings bearing the date some of the third, very many of the tenth century; to enter the ancient town-hall, of the latter period, interesting besides from its frescoed ceilings and the historical pictures which adorned its walls; the room, still a royal residence, in which Luther read out the Augsburg confession to Charles V.; the cloister in which he lived for ten days, and the adjoining church in which he sometimes preached; to go over the houses of the Fugger family,—the Rothschilds of the seventeenth century; to see that mansion, from the window of which, Philippina Welser, the fair maid of Augsburg, captivated the heart of the heir of the Holy Roman Empire; to examine the little chapel in the hotel Drei Mohren, kept still in precisely the same condition as when the Emperor Charles V. heard mass there; and the room, now sadly desecrated, in which the generous Fugger burned in a cinnamon fire, in the presence of the Emperor, the bond given him by that prince for the heavy sums advanced by him for the expenses of the war against the Moors; to enjoy, too, the sight of water playing from fountains of ancient date and classic form. All these attractive objects—not to speak of others of more modern construction—constitute the charm of Augsburg, and make it, next to Nuremberg, which stands *facile princeps*, the most interesting of the old cities of Germany.

The railway journey from Augsburg to Lindau on Lake Constance took about six hours. Its weariness was broken by the peculiar conversation of an Englishman in the carriage, who, unable to speak German, and being somewhat overbearing in his manners, had been terribly fleeced in Austria and Hungary, and who favoured his fellow-travellers with his experiences. Suddenly and accidentally the conversation turned on the French emperor, and then the Englishman's excitement knew no bounds. He endorsed all Kinglake's attacks, and painted him in the most odious colours, with the manifest sympathy of the Germans in the carriage who understood him, and with whom Louis Napoleon was no favourite. But when the Englishman diverted his attacks to Germany, the smiles on the faces of his companions disappeared, and it was easy to see that the subject was unpalatable to them. With great forbearance, however, they allowed him to rattle on. Lindau was reached that evening, and left on the following morning, our travellers embarking on board the steamer at 7 A.M. The day was lovely; the scenery, however, on the shores of Lake Constance is not very interesting. It is a small inland sea, some idea of the length of which may be obtained from the fact that to proceed from the most eastern point of Bregenz to the point beyond Constance where the Rhine is entered, a steamer requires seven hours. A distant view is obtained from the decks of the steamer of the giants of Switzerland, but the German side of the lake is almost flat. After the Rhine is entered the scenery improves. On a prettily wooded height may be seen the castle of Arenenberg, the property of the Emperor Napoleon, the scene in which he passed his infant years, from whence he undertook his Strasbourg expedition, and in which he closed his mother's eyes. Here, apparently, the feeling towards the former inmate of the castle is much more favourable than in Germany.

Schaffhausen reached about 4 P.M., our travellers started at once for a little inn called the Hotel Witzig, situated on the railway, and about a quarter of a mile from the falls. This hotel had been strongly recommended to them, and they found it most comfortable. Scarcely had they secured a room in it when they set out again to see the falls which make the Schaffhausen famous. Most wonderful are they! Such a volume of water; such a breadth; such a mass of foam! As they stood underneath the fall, in a sort of arbour, just at the head of the Rhine, it was impossible for them, looking up, to see the summit of the crest; the waves seemed as though about to overwhelm and sweep them away. The sight of this mass of water, enjoyed from the particular point—and it is the tourist's point—was quite sufficient to extort the most unfeigned admiration. There are, nevertheless, mockers who deride it. More to be envied, we think, are those to whom is left the faculty of enjoyment, who are able to bear willing and heart-felt testimony to the wonders and glories of nature, who are neither too wrapt up in themselves, nor in their own fancied importance, to be pleased!

From Schaffhausen the Musafirs proceeded next morning to Lucerne, arriving there about mid-day. We will not dwell upon the meeting with Punjaubee, or the introduction to his wife and her family. It will suffice to say that a very short time induced a feeling amongst all the members of the party that their acquaintance had been not for hours but for years. Shame on those Anglo-Indians who malign their countrymen by imputing to them unnatural coldness and reserve; never was there a more stupid calumny uttered! The fault is not in the English; the fault is with those Anglo-Indians, who, descending from a position of colonial importance to one of equality with their fellow-countrymen, cannot bring themselves to accept the reality of their new *status*, but sigh in vain for the adulation to which, as leaders of society, they have been accustomed in India! We have always regarded it as a strong mark of common sense the admission from a lady in India, more especially a lady in high position, that she prefers England to India. The temptation to a certain order of mind to prefer India is so strong, that there are really many who are unable to resist it. Miss Edgeworth once wrote a very famous tale, in which she pourtrayed the struggles of a tradesman's wife to migrate from the first position in Cranbourne Alley to the last in Bedford Row, and painted in glowing terms the misery of her position when she got there. There is a moral in the story, the application of which, taken either in its natural sense or inversely, commends itself to very many in India.

For our parts, and judging simply from the personal experience gained from two successive visits to the old country, we hesitate not to declare our conviction that the English people proper are the kindest, the most hospitable, the warmest-hearted people in the world. They must know who you are before they will receive you into their houses; but, satisfied on that point, the Anglo-Indian may be sure that he will be received on his own merits and be judged accordingly. As a rule, in fact, the only disagreeable people we met in England were the Anglo-Indians settled there. Many of them were so wrapped up in themselves, and in the bygone glories of their former days, so satisfied that every Englishman they met in the street knew they were Anglo-Indians, and therefore intended to slight them, that they were quite intolerable. We write thus as much in warning as in sober earnest. We are jealous of the character of our Anglo-Indians. We are vexed that they should be regarded, that they should regard themselves, as a race apart, distinct from the great body of their countrymen. We are desirous, above all, that they should rid themselves of the foolish notion, in many of them quite rampant, that they are more learned and wise than the bulk of the Englishmen they are brought in contact with. We much fear that this feeling is one of the main causes of the line they take up. They are not appreciated according to their fancied merits; they seek for refuge, therefore, in the reminiscences of the past, and shut their eyes to the present.

But to return to the Musafirs. After many rambles with Punjaubee and his relations in the neighbourhood of Lucerne; after ascending the Bürgenstock, "doing" Pilatus, and walking over the other hills which surround the glorious lake, it was determined to make an excursion to one of the snow mountains, thence to proceed to Interlaken, and from that place across the Wengern Alp to the glaciers of Grindelwald and Rosenlaui. The route is an oft-trodden one, but the adventures met with by some of the party render it worthy of a notice in this faithful record of Captain Musafir's wanderings.

The snow mountain fixed upon was the Titlis, nearly 11,000 feet high. To reach it from Lucerne the traveller had to proceed to Stanzstadt at the other end of the lake, thence to the village Stantz, and from there to Engelberg. At Engelberg began the regular ascent, across the Joch Pass, to a little inn on the Engstlen Alp. From this the ascent of the Titlis was generally made.

As at that time of the year, the month of August, the Engstlen Alp inn was often crowded with tourists, it was deemed a wise and even a necessary precaution that the landlord of that inn should be written to, in order that rooms might be secured for the whole party. As, however, the necessity for such a step did not present itself until it was too late to receive an answer at Lucerne, the landlord was requested to direct his reply to the inn at Engelberg, in which, in case he should be full, the travellers hoped to find quarters for the night. All these arrangements having been completed, the party, consisting of Musafir and his wife, Punjaubee, his wife, her two sisters, and her brother, stepped on board a steamer at Lucerne. A merrier one never set out on any expedition. A French writer not long ago alluded to the charming and graceful facility with which English girls adapt themselves to all the circumstances of travel; how their gay and sprightly laughter quadruples the pleasure of climbing up the mountain side: how they may be seen adorning the loftiest peaks, how thus daring and enduring of fatigue in the mountains, they are, when met again in the drawing-room, as graceful and natural in another way; totally without affectation and without too great self-esteem; always anxious to please, yet never overstepping the bounds of true feminine reserve. After describing their charming manners, so happily adapted to all circumstances, in a vein of chivalrous enthusiasm, he gravely adds: " Some people complain of the English as being a nation of travellers; but I would soberly inquire, what would those mountains be without those charming, high-spirited girls, whose coloured petticoats may be always seen in contrast, now to the green mountain side, now to the snowy peak; who have a kind word for every stranger who may speak to them; whose merry laughter disperses the gloomiest atmosphere, and inspires a whole company; who climb to delight themselves, and who succeed in delighting all around them. Miserable would be the man who, having made one visit to the mountains in such society, should go there a second time to find that they were absent."

If the words we have quoted had not been written before the period of Musafir's visit, we should have believed that the chivalrous Frenchman must have belonged to one of the many parties that interchanged civilities with the merry travellers whose short tour we are about to describe. Certainly in gay and airy spirits, in the enjoyment of the little difficulties which beset travellers, in thorough appreciation of lovely scenery, in sprightly humour, in amiability and kind-heartedness, and the most entire abnegation of self upon every occasion, these ladies realised the description we have quoted. Without such, a tour of this sort must be a blank, with them it is the most perfect enjoyment.

The travellers left Lucerne at 8 o'clock in the morning in a steamer for the little village of Stanzstadt, where they hoped to find carriages to take them on. Here, however, they met with their first mishap, which led indirectly to all those that followed. Not a carriage was available. There had, they were informed, been a great rush that day to Engelberg, and every conveyance had been taken up. Still as it was only a distance of three miles to Stanz, which was a much larger place, it was easy to walk there. They started accordingly, their traps being conveyed in a sort of wheelbarrow. An hour took them to Stanz, but here too there were some difficulties about carriages; so, to while away the time whilst these were being smoothed away, they rambled over the place, and looked at the church and other lions. At the end of about a couple of hours two carriages were produced, and in these they set out for Engelberg. The day was lovely though very hot indeed. As there was now no prospect of reaching Engelberg before 5 o'clock, and they had a foot journey of five hours to the Engstlen Alp after that, our travellers took the opportunity of arriving at a very pretty spot to dine *al fresco*. They then pushed on, but as from that point to Engelberg the ascent was rather steep, Musafir and Punjaubee's brother-in-law—whom we shall call Oxonian—walked it, and arrived at Engelberg nearly an hour before the carriages. In reply to their inquiries they found that every room in the inns and *pensions* in Engelberg was occupied, that not a pony was to be had to take the ladies on to the Engstlen Alp, and that there were but two *chaises à porteur*, one of them broken, and which it would take an hour to repair. To compensate for this, however, a letter was found from the landlord of the Engstlen Alp inn to the address of Musafir, stating that he had secured rooms for his party.

It was now 5 o'clock, and as the carriages were believed to be close behind, an order was issued for the immediate repair of the second chair, and guides and porters were called out with the utmost despatch. Still it was 6 o'clock before the carriages arrived, and half-past that hour before the two chaises with the proper complement of porters and luggage-bearers were ready to start. They had then, as we have said, a five hours' march before them, over very steep ground, as after passing a very high point in front of Engelberg, they had to descend to the Trüb See—a most dismal place—and from that to ascend the Joch Pass (7,244 feet), from the summit of which the Engstlen Alp was nearly four miles distant. However, the journey and its difficulties were made light of in anticipation, and at half-past 6 they started, the three gentlemen walking, and the four ladies using the chairs alternately.

It was a lovely evening, but unfortunately there was no

moon. For half an hour the seven travellers pushed on rapidly, but then came the ascent of the steep point which separates Engelberg from the Joch Pass. Still, laughing, talking, stopping to gaze at the lovely scenery which makes Engelberg so popular, they trudged steadily on. But before that first ascent had been achieved, daylight had disappeared, and even the twilight was fast fading. Then came the descent to the Trüb See,—a flat sandy surface interspersed with watercourses, which it was difficult in the dark to cross without getting wet. However, the various members of the party progressed somehow by the aid of mutual assistance, and all re-united at a châlet in the depths of the Trüb See. This châlet bore a striking contrast to the Alm-hütte of Austria, being not only dirty itself, but apparently the cause of dirt in its inmates. Nevertheless hunger overpowered other considerations, and the seven did not scruple to partake of bread and milk, albeit offered them by not the cleanest of hands, and charged for—again in contrast to Austria—exorbitantly. It was now close upon 9 o'clock, and pitch dark. The lanterns were therefore lighted, and the travellers, refreshed, set out again for the ascent of the Joch Pass. They had not, however, gone very far before all the lights, except one tallow candle, went out, the guides lost their way, members of the party got separated, and confusion became worse confounded. There remained only to all the consciousness that there was a steep ascent before them, and that they had to climb it. How they wandered, and fell, and tumbled, how this one rolled down an incline, and the other scrambled amongst the rocks, boots not to describe; it was certainly rough work, but had it been ten times more so, he would have been worse than a heathen who had not enjoyed it, supported, as all were, by the imperturbable merriment and good humour of those brave English girls. What though they fell, they got up again with a jest; what though the ascent seemed never ending, they were always to the fore; what though even the guides murmured, they made light of every difficulty. It was really an inspiring sight to watch those girls, who in a drawing-room would have attracted all by their grace and elegance, meet thus lightly the difficulties of a night march in a region of snow-clad mountains, not knowing one inch of the way, and the guides floundering in darkness. Still on they went, merrily and cheerfully, until at last the summit of the Joch Pass was stumbled upon rather than reached. It was very cold, the snow lying within a few feet of them, albeit not directly on their path, and though now past midnight, they had yet four miles to traverse. Once on the summit, the track to the Engstlen Alp was soon found, and they pushed on merrily, descending in the four miles about 1,200 feet. This distance was accomplished in something over the hour, and about half-past 1 o'clock they entered the little inn on the Engstlen Alp, having walked for seven hours since leaving Engelberg. But the catastrophe of their adventures was at hand. There was naturally no one at that hour waiting their arrival, but a light was burning in the kitchen, and to it they bent their steps, Musafir leading the way. On opening the door they encountered the landlord, rather a smart-looking man, ready dressed; the cook, too, was busy at the fire, and there were no signs of turning-in. At their appearance the landlord appeared at first startled and surprised; but when Musafir, addressing him in German, told him that they formed the party regarding whom he had addressed a letter to the hotel at Engelberg, the form of his visage began strangely to alter. He did not speak, but an expression of sadness and self-reproach replaced that of astonishment. For some short time he did no more than stand still and wring his hands. By this time all the seven were assembled in the kitchen, curiously watching the apparently insane motions of the host. In vain did Musafir and Oxonian address him: he would not speak, but continued to hang out signals of distress with his hands. At last, the form of the question was varied, and Musafir asked him for their rooms. But this query seemed only to redouble his grief; at last, making a tremendous effort, he exclaimed: "I kept the rooms for you till 10 o'clock; the influx of guests then was so great and your arrival was so uncertain, that I was forced then to give them up. Yes," added the poor fellow, "and I've given up my own room too,—this is the place where I have to sleep." With these words he opened a cupboard showing a mattress stretched on the floor. The feelings of our travellers on hearing these words found vent in a loud and prolonged and hearty laugh. There was something so novel in being in such a position after a seven hours' walk, something to them so enjoyable, that they sat down on the bench in the kitchen and roared. The landlord at first could not believe his senses. He looked from one member of the party to the other as if he doubted whether their mirth was genuine; then at himself as if sceptical of his own existence. It was doubtless new to him to hear guests suddenly deprived of their rooms meet him, not with reproaches, but with merriment. At last he, too, was carried away, and added his own laughter to the others! When this outbreak had somewhat subsided, the idea began to steal over the intruding visitors that they were hungry. They, therefore, took the opportunity of restored quiet to ask the landlord whether he could give them something to eat. His face brightened up at the question as he replied, looking towards the blazing fire : " Oh yes, what will you have ? " Almost immediately afterwards, however, his countenance fell, as he exclaimed, " But we 've no room to serve it in." " Can't we have it in the *salle à manger* ? " asked one of the party. " Well," said the host ruefully, " I have a *salle à manger*, but there are three Englishmen sleeping in it, and the door is locked." Our travellers, however, were not to be baulked of their meal by the idea of encountering three *Engländer*, as the host called them, and it was resolved that one of their party should accompany the latter to hold a parley with their countrymen. For this duty Oxonian was selected. The two set forth and knocked at the door of the room, but for some time knocked in vain. At last, however, the knocks became louder, and a movement was heard within. After some consultation the door was opened, the two ambassadors entered, when to his surprise Oxonian recognised in the three *Engländer* three relatives, one of them a young cousin whom we will designate as " Cantab." The parley at once assumed a pleasant aspect, and an agreement, fair to both, was soon entered into between the two high contracting parties. It was decided that one end of the room, which was a long one, should be kept in utter darkness, and that in this end the three gentlemen should continue to repose, that the other end should be brilliantly lighted up, and at this the ladies should sup. This arrangement entered into, the countenance of the landlord assumed a benignant hue, and he incited his cook to exert herself to the utmost. This she did, and in about half an hour a most excellent supper was served up, to which ample justice was rendered by the travellers, good digestion waiting on appetite, health on both, and, to borrow a simile from the immortal Dickens,—the smiling landlord upon all three. Certainly a merrier party never sat down anywhere to a meal.

With the discovery by Oxonian of his three relatives, the fortunes of our travellers appear to have taken a turn. For no sooner was their jovial supper over, and the question had begun to be mooted as to what they should do next, than two Germans leaving one of the bedrooms, entered the *salle* bent upon ascending the Titlis. "At least the ladies can now be provided for," whispered the landlord to Musafir, as he instantly gave orders for the room to be swept out and the beds made ready. Of these there were but three, and there were four ladies, but it was not difficult to arrange for the remainder of the night. The three gentlemen meanwhile made themselves comfortable on the floor.

The next day some of the inmates of the little inn went away and all our travellers were accommodated. The landlord, however, never forgot the good humour with which they had borne what he believed they would regard as a great disappointment. He treated them henceforth as his most honoured guests, and exhausted all his resources to make them feel perfectly at home. The kindness was appreciated although the exertions were scarcely needed, for with such a party and in such a lovely spot he would have been a yahoo indeed who could have been in the least degree put out.

The Engstlen Alp is, indeed, one of Nature's favourite spots. About 6,000 feet above the level of the sea, it is surrounded by glorious mountains, some of them white masses of snow. Others again wear a grassy covering until just at the very summit. Close to the inn is a little lake formed of glacier water, which, though icy cold, was infinitely refreshing after a day's excursion. Between the inn and the mountains are smaller elevations, prettily wooded, and containing numberless species of wild flowers, some of them rare, whilst the road in the valley descending to Imhof follows the course of a most beautiful little river, running over rocks, and abounding in cascades and waterfalls, which appear to the greater advantage from the luxuriant foliage on the other side.

The day after their arrival at the little inn was spent in wandering amongst these scenes, and most delightful it was to revel in the bright snow, and gaze as one could over many miles of mountains whose dazzling peaks had soared on high for centuries, then to descend into the valley and admire the charming contrast of wild and luxuriant foliage, to crown all by a plunge into the ice-cold lake. At about 4 o'clock, the Germans who had ascended the Titlis returned. They gave a most melancholy account of their trip, described it as not only difficult but dangerous, and they strongly advised our travellers not to think of attempting it, one of them showing the cuts and bruises he had received in a fall which, he seemed to think, might have been fatal. This advice was entirely thrown away on the male portion of our travellers, but it had possibly some effect in deciding them not to allow the ladies to join the party,—a decision which was entirely opposed to their inclinations.

At one o'clock on the following morning, the four gentlemen —Oxonian, Cantab, Punjaubee, and Musafir—were roused from their slumbers, and partaking, after dressing, of a slight meal, started off to make the ascent of the Titlis. They again walked to the summit of the Joch Pass, then descending to the right, crossed a glacier at the foot of the Titlis, and then began the ascent. After climbing for about two hours they reached a point just below the level of the snow. Here they stopped and breakfasted. After a short rest they again started, and going as it were round the mountain under the snow level, reached the point from which they were again to mount. Here, as they were to enter the snow, they were roped together, thus :—a guide first, the Punjaubee, Cantab, Oxonian, Musafir, guide. At first the snow was hard, but as the sun's power became stronger and stronger, it soon became so soft as to cause each climber to plunge in it above the knee. They passed several crevasses, seemingly without foundation of any sort, but their guides knew the road well, and steered them clear of them all. Ahead of them, at one time the distance of nearly an hour, was a party of foreigners also accompanied by two guides. On these our friends steadily gained, and when within 200 yards of the summit, closed with them. A tremendous race now ensued, both parties walking their best. It ended, however, by a few seconds in favour of the travellers whose adventures we are tracing.

The ascent achieved, all the pedestrians sat still to gaze at the glorious view which presented itself from the summit of the mountain. Some lovely peaks lay but a few hundred feet above their level; beneath them a sea of snow, broken up as it were into waves, so irregular were the formations; above them the clear blue heaven, its glory undiminished by a single cloud, and all around them the crisp fresh air, wonderfully exhilarating, and taking away all sense of fatigue. It was a most enjoyable half-hour, and if one thought did occur to affect it, it was that the ladies, who might easily, as it turned out, have made the ascent, were not there to partake of and to heighten their pleasure.

The descent of our friends was very rapid: the snow was melting more and more every minute, and they consequently made all haste to reach the point below it. Thence they went on more leisurely, and meeting some of the ladies near the Joch Pass, they proceeded at an easy pace, reaching the Alp just eleven hours after they had left it. One or two of them felt rather tired, but a plunge into the glacier water of the lake took away every vestige of fatigue. Indeed, so little did two out of the four feel the ascent, that Punjaubee declared that if he had been alone he could have done it in an hour less time, whilst Oxonian actually did climb again to the summit the following morning in company with some friends who unexpectedly arrived that evening.

The following morning, the whole party, now reduced to six by the defection of Oxonian, separated from their other friends and from their jovial host, and started for Brienz. The parting with the host was quite affecting so much had he taken to our friends. He begged them to return, and promised that whatever might happen there should always be room for them. The walk from Engstlen to Imhof, along the course of the little river before referred to, was most lovely, and many were the additions made to the collections of ferns and wild flowers. It was like strolling through a beautiful park, so soft was the turf, so beautiful the trees, and so enchanting the entire scenery. Indeed, what with the ferns and the wild strawberries, and halts in beautiful spots, our travellers delayed somewhat too long upon the road, so that by the time they reached Imhof, at a considerable lower elevation than Engstlen, the sun was shining with a power that made itself felt. Here, too, no carriages were available for some time for a start to Brienz, and it was 7 P.M. before they could get away; 10 o'clock before they reached their destination.

Brienz, a rather uninteresting town at the northernmost end of the lake which bears its name, is the point of embarkation for Interlaken, at the other end, to which place our travellers proceeded on the following morning, halting there a day, and making, amongst other excursions, a visit to the famous falls of Giesbach. These, though very beautiful, are not, according to Musafir, equal in interest to the waterfall of Golling, which the unexplored mystery of the imprisoned lake within the mountain invests with a kind of romance unattainable by any other he had seen. The following morning they all started for the Wengern Alp.

We will not attempt to follow our travellers in the further details of their tour. We leave them in ground well known to the tourists, and which the majority of our readers have probably explored for themselves. It will suffice to state that passing Lauterbrunnen and the famous **fall, the Staubbach,** they crossed the Wengern Alp, sat for some hours *vis-à-vis* to those glories of Switzerland, the **Jung-frau with her** two horns, the Silberhorn and **the Schneehorn, the Mönch,** and the Eiger, listening **to** the descending **avalanches, and** watching the striking effect of the alternate sunshine and cloud on their hoary heads; then, passing over the little Scheideck (6,788 feet), the weather bitterly cold, they descended **in a storm of** thunder and lightning to Grindelwald; that **there** they visited, the following day, its famous glacier, **and walked on** its sea of ice, being out all day on the trip, and returning wet through; that, **the next day, they crossed** the upper Scheideck, **having** previously done honour to a little grotto hewn **out of** pure ice on the **upper glacier of** Grindelwald; then descending to Rosenlaui, **famous for its** lovely ferns, they visited **its glacier, and pushed on** the **same** evening to **Reichenbach. As the weather had now set in rainy** they deemed **it wise to curtail their** expedition, **and to return** over the Brünig Pass—an **uninteresting route—to** Lucerne, the rain coming down in torrents **all the way. It was a most** enjoyable trip, without **one drawback from its** beginning to its close, except perhaps the **wet** weather **after** passing the Scheideck; but even **the** dismal state **of the sky** brought into more striking contrast **the cheerfulness and gaiety of the companions of Musafir.**

A few days later it cleared up again, and **another trip was** attempted. Of this too, equally enjoyable **as the first, we** shall merely give **the** outline. Starting **early one morning they steamed to Flüelen,** passing **Tell's chapel** *en route*, **then drove to Amstag, passing through the village of Altorf, the** scene of many of the exploits of the far-famed patriot of Switzerland. Sleeping at Amstag, they started at four o'clock next morning for a walk up the Maderaner Thal to the Hüfi glacier at its further end. This walk is one of the most beautiful in Switzerland. The "Thal," or valley, runs up between two ranges of mountains, those on the one side covered with lovely foliage, those on the other, bare, grand, and imposing. The valley between these two is most beautiful, consisting of alternate mead and forest, with a picturesque brook below, crossed more than once by the most picturesque of bridges. All the members of the party were, as usual, in the highest spirits and eager for a climb. Breakfasting *en route*, the Hüfi glacier was reached about mid-day. It is a glorious glacier, full of crevasses, a glance down which shows one the ice clear and transparent to a very great depth. After disporting themselves on this glacier for some time, they all returned to Amstag after a most enjoyable trip.

Next day, starting in carriages, they drove up the St. Gothard Pass as far as Hospenthal. It was a glorious drive; indeed, under no circumstances could it have been otherwise, but on this occasion the day was most favourable, and the mountain foliage, the rugged rocks, the winding turns, were seen to the very best advantage. The same evening they returned to Lucerne, and a few days later the Musafirs bade adieu to their friends and to Switzerland, carrying away with them an immense appreciation of the English as a people,— an appreciation which further experience in England tended only to confirm and to increase.

From Lucerne the Musafirs travelled direct, *viâ* Strasbourg, to the Black Forest, to enjoy in it a month's ramble. We shall not follow them so far, but part with them at Strasbourg, where Musafir, who, even at the time of the imprisonment of the heir of the empire in Ham,—where he wrote these words: " With the name I bear there are only two destinies which are proper to me, a prison or a throne,"—had watched his career with interest,—seized the opportunity of inspecting the spot where he made his abortive attempt in 1836. The place where Louis Napoleon was taken prisoner is a narrow piece of ground in front of the Infantry barracks, bounded on the other side by a wall. It was this narrowness of space that was fatal to him. At the head of the artillery, which had pronounced for him at once, he had gone along a narrow street leading to the Infantry barracks, and, passing between these, had found himself in the narrow space above referred to, the mass of the artillery remaining in the street outside. When in the narrow space, the soldiers crowded out of the barracks to listen to the harangue addressed to them by Louis Napoleon. They were just about to declare for him when the colonel of the regiment, by name Tallandier, rushed forward, and said to his men—" You think you are going to declare for the heir of Napoleon; this is not he, this is an impostor, a son of Colonel Vaudry." This readiness on the part of Tallandier had the effect he wished for. The soldiers saw in the features of the young man before them no resemblance to the features of the first emperor. Colonel Tallandier's confidence of assertion added to their doubts, and they, who would have marched to Paris for the nephew of the Emperor, declined to have aught to do with an impostor. There is little doubt in the present day that but for that speech of Tallandier the plot would have succeeded. Musafir was assured that all the regiments on the eastern frontier had been gained, and needed but the signal from Strasbourg to rally to the Napoleonic standard. It is, perhaps, better as it is. The emperor owes much to his six years of silence and meditation in the castle of Ham.

We have now brought to a conclusion the rough notes with which we have been entrusted by Captain Musafir. They tell but a plain and unvarnished story; but if the perusal of that story incite others to reserve themselves for the intense pleasure, whilst yet they are able to enjoy it, of European travel; if it induce them to shake off local prejudices and to conform as much as may be to the standard prevalent in Europe; if it persuade them to see and judge for themselves whether their countrymen in Europe are so cold and distant as they are sometimes represented to be by resident Anglo-Indians, we shall not regret the trouble of the compilation, for we shall then feel that we have accomplished a real success.

We will only add that Captain Musafir has promised to send us the notes he took of a pedestrian journey in the Salzkammergut and Tirol the year subsequent to the adventures we have recorded. Should they appear after examination to be of a nature to enlist the interest of the public, we shall endeavour to prepare them for a future number.

III.

THE requests which have reached us on the subject, from very many quarters, induce us to lay before the public the third and last division of Captain Musafir's tour in the mountains of Europe. We do so with the less regret, because we regard the subject as pre-eminently fraught with interest to Anglo-Indians. Those who have passed the best part of their lives in India, and to whom Europe appears in the same light as did the promised land to the wearied followers of Moses ere yet Pisgah was reached and the waters of the Jordan left behind, are particularly anxious to learn from the experience of travelled Anglo-Indians, what they must do, where they should go, what preparations are necessary for the journey, the capabilities of the countries which they must traverse, the habits of European life, the expenses of travelling, its discomforts and advantages. Now, we need scarcely repeat that we do not write for those whose sole, or whose chief, object in life is what is called "society,"—a phrase which we take to signify shabby-gentility of the highest order,—a sort of life in which each family vies with its neighbour in profusion of outward show, and in which the giving and attending formal dinner-parties, with their necessary concomitants of late hours and heating stimulants, appear the end and aim of being. Such a life as this, with its many variations, its natural fostering of superficial accomplishments, and its tendency to emasculate the mind, has always appeared to us to be a waste of existence. For those congenial spirits whom it suits these pages are not written. We address ourselves solely to those who love nature in her endless varieties of matchless beauty, who prefer the green slopes of the mountain sides to the waxed floor of the ballroom, the glorious sunrise to the glare of gas-lamps, and the sparkling water of the mountain stream to the peculiar compound which too often does duty for champagne. For these and these alone we string together the rough notes of Captain Musafir. In a perusal of his travels they will find at least some indication of the pleasures which wandering over the Alpine regions opens out to the manly mind; they will see that it requires little money and that it entails little trouble to find enjoyment unsurpassed anywhere in the world; and, seeing this, they will think it no deprivation to abstain from costly and unsatisfactory indulgences in this country, in order the more thoroughly to avail themselves, when they are able to take to their furlough, of the rich enjoyment of European travel.

It has been suggested to us by more than one of those who have expressed an interest in the previous account of Captain Musafir's wandering, that we should endeavour to add to the practical character of the narrative by stating in a detailed form the proper outfit of a traveller, the amount of baggage to which he should confine himself, and the expenses of the route. It is our intention to respond as fully as we can to this invitation, and, as we hold very strongly the opinion that the pleasures of travelling, great at all times, are immensely enhanced by the society of ladies, we shall make our remarks on this head applicable to both sexes. We shall indicate the nature and number of the dresses each ought to carry, and shall point out the means by which those who are accustomed to the unlimited amplitude of an Indian wardrobe may be induced to restrict their requirements to the simple necessities of the traveller. In fact we hope to make this paper practically useful to the Anglo-Indians of the class for which it is written.

But before we enter on this part of the subject we shall lay before our readers, from Captain Musafir's notes, his account of his tour in Tirol and the mountains adjacent. It was but a simple walk of a month's duration, taken in company with a friend. But though simple, it was beyond description enjoyable. In fact its simplicity constituted one of its chief charms. To see the mountain-peasants in all the vivid reality of unsophisticated life, courteous, friendly, hospitable, fond of strangers, anxious to please, unspoilt by a pseudo-civilization, neither grasping nor reserved, but in the highest sense of the term enjoying existence, going to their work in the morning with zest and returning from it with a light heart, ready to join in the rustic dance, or to listen to the sound of the guitar, its strings deftly struck by the hands of some village maiden;—to see them, happy and contented, never uproarious or drunken, satisfied with little, never happier than when hired to assist a gentleman in his pursuit of the chamois, or to accompany him in a crusade against the finny tribes;—to see them thus, is a sight now, alas! only to be witnessed in Austria and Tirol,—countries in which no over-pressure of a selfish civilization has produced rudeness of speech and sullenness of conduct, and where, as yet, associations for licensed murder, such as those which have lately been exposed at Sheffield, are, thank God, unknown and impossible. Of all the European races, indeed, there are none who in manly symmetry of form, and in womanly beauty, in hearty, honest simplicity of life and manners, and in natural refinement and warm-heartedness, can bear comparison with the peasantry of Upper and Lower Austria, Styria, Carinthia' Carniola, and Tirol. In this part of the world the traveller, if he be not himself a boor, can enjoy the best and finest of all those blessings which make this earth so bright; he sees the most glorious scenery, not surpassed by Switzerland; he can wander over paths, accessible to all, and of wonderful loveliness; he need take with him only a few clothes, for everything else he finds provided in the cleanest of inns by the most civil of hosts; he has abundant society, for the conversation of the peasants is a mine of gold,—not to speak of the travellers constantly met with; music is there a national passion; sport of all sorts is abundant; civility and kindliness are Austrian habits. To enjoy all this it is only necessary that the traveller should be capable of enjoyment; that he should not have been spoiled by artificial manners and that over-refinement of civilization which can see nothing good in a foreigner; that he should conform to national customs and meet politeness with its like. For a man who can do this, and who understands the language of the country, those provinces are a Paradise.

Captain Musafir's last tour was necessarily limited in point of time. He, alas! had within six weeks of its conclusion to set out once more for his Indian home, and he could spare but one month for the final peep at the country which, during his wanderings of the previous year, he had learned so much to love. It was impossible therefore to traverse the whole of it. Much that is beautiful and lovely has therefore been left for another visit to Europe. Bearing in mind the time available, it was determined by him, in consultation with the friend who was to be his companion, and whom we will call Mercator, to walk first over the Salzkammergut; then, after a glance at the König's See, to proceed southwards to Wildbad Gastein; crossing thence the Rauriser Taurn to Windish Matrey to make their way *via* Meran to Innsbruck, thence through the Finstermünz Pass, and over the Stelvio into Italy as far as Tirano; from that place across the Bernina into the glorious valley of the Engadin,—the head-quarters of the Alpine Club,—and thence *via* Chur and Ragatz to Zurich, where the tour would end. A glance at the map will show the excellence of the plan, and though the weather, as we shall see, prevented its being carried out in its entirety, its main features were yet substantially adhered to throughout.

The two travellers met at Salzburg on the morning of the 4th August. In proceeding to that place Musafir took the opportunity of stopping at and inspecting the fine old town of Bamberg, and of renewing his acquaintance with

Nuremberg, which he had visited five years before. Both these cities, the symbols of a bygone era, are most interesting. Though very near to one another,—the distance being but thirty-eight miles,—they were respectively, during the religious wars of the seventeenth century, the head-quarters of the rival parties in Bavaria—the free city of Nuremberg being firmly and exclusively Protestant, whilst the archiepiscopal Bamberg was rooted in its attachment to the ancient faith. In this respect they are altered only in so far that they are less exclusive and more liberal; for Bamberg still retains its Romanist character, whilst in Nuremberg, out of a population of 60,000, there are but 4,000 who are not Protestants. Of the two cities Nuremberg claims the attention to a far greater degree than the other. Once within its walls, the traveller lives, as it were, in the sixteenth century, when it was one of the chief cities of Europe, and its fame was in every land. The picturesque streets with their gabled houses still bearing the ancient sign-boards; the magnificent churches, uninjured, though Nuremberg became reformed, during the Reformation; the fine old castle on the hill overlooking the town, glorious from its still stately appearance and from its many reminiscences,—for not only was it the ancient seat of the Hohenzollerns, but from its towers the great Gustavus watched the blockading army of Wallenstein, and from it he sallied to fight his first great battle with the leader whom he was yet destined to beat, though in beating to die. The monuments of Peter Vischer and of Adam Krafft; the paintings of Albert Durer; and, perhaps more than all, the unmistakable assertion of former glories apparent in every street, in every building, in the lofty demeanour of the inhabitants;—all these are wonderfully impressive. The genius of the place asserts itself everywhere. The stranger is under an influence such as no other city is capable of producing. The magnificence of a past era appeals irresistibly to the spell-bound imagination. The admiration excited by every striking portion of the old town is mingled with reverence and awe; and when he does tear himself away, he is sensible not merely of departure from one place to another, but of a return to the world of the present.

Those who should visit Nuremberg and Bamberg intent upon other objects than merely the inspection of both cities, would do well to remember that they form two angles of a triangle, of which the third angle is Baireuth, containing a most charming district, full of hills and rivers, fossil caves and lovely scenery, known as Franconian Switzerland. Ten days or a fortnight can well be spent in rambling over this most lovely district, equally attractive to the fisherman, the geologist, and the lover of scenery. The trout and grayling fishing is really most excellent, and can easily be procured. Nine years ago Musafir went over a part of this district with some relatives, and he has to this day a vivid recollection, not only of the lovely scenery, but of the excellent fishing properties of the numerous clear and rapid rivers which he met with in his travels. There is consolation in the thought that it is a country which will well repay a second visit.

Leaving Nuremberg, Musafir proceeded by rail to Munich. Starting from that place early on the following morning he met Mercator at the railway station, and they travelled in the same train to Salzburg, putting up there at the hotel, visited by Musafir the previous year, known as the Drei Alliirten, kept by the obliging Mr. Jung. Again were the salient points of this most striking town visited and admired; the two hills, which add so much to its beauty, on either side of the Salza, ascended, our travellers stopping on the summit of the Capuzinerberg till the view it commanded— that of the castle surmounting the town in the foreground, with the Untersberg, Watzmann, and other glorious mountains behind it—became deeply impressed on their memory. Returning thence to the inn, making on their way the necessary arrangements regarding the exchange of their English gold into Austrian paper, they found that Mr. Jung, true to his reputation, had already procured a guide, who agreed to conduct them as far as the lake called the Mond See, eighteen miles distant, the following morning. Having settled with this needful companion, they asked Mr. Jung how they could spend the evening pleasantly. "Oh," he replied, "why not go to the open-air concert;—entrance free, and the best band in Salzburg." Thither accordingly, after dinner, they proceeded. We record the fact merely to show the pleasant, easily amused, orderly nature of the Austrian people. The two Englishmen entered a large piece of ground enclosed all around, and capable of containing thousands. On a raised platform near the entrance was a magnificent Austrian band. Beyond this the ground was nearly covered with little tables, fitted each to accommodate from two to eight persons, with as many chairs. At these tables were the population of Salzburg of all grades. Some had before them ices, some coffee, some wine, but the majority beer and cheese. In fact almost all belonged to the artizan class. But there they sat, so quietly, so orderly, and yet listening intently to the music; giving vent to their feelings only in a tremendous *Hoch*,* when some favourite or national air touched a chord in their hearts. Between the performances, they went to their beer, or talked good-humouredly with one another. The band, as are most Austrian bands, was magnificent. It was a sight peculiarly Austrian. The people of this nation possess an instinctive love of simple pleasures, and never allow their spirits to carry them into excesses. At Vienna, they almost jostle the Emperor in the gardens of Schönbrunn and on the Prater. There is no attempt to incommode their sovereign by crowding round him and staring at him; but with true politeness they allow him to pass as one of themselves. At Salzburg this audience of artizans conducted themselves with as much order and propriety, and with as true an appreciation of music, as could have the most aristocratic society at a concert in the Hanover Square rooms.

On the following morning the tour commenced. Each traveller was armed with a small bag, containing the wardrobe necessary for a walking expedition,—the nature of which will be hereafter described,—an umbrella, a light overcoat, and a stick or Alpine stock. The bag was of such a size that it might easily have been carried by the traveller in case of necessity. Practically, however, both bags were always carried by the guide, it being a service to which men

* The Austrian Hurrah.

of that class are accustomed. We have said that an arrangement had been made with one of these men to conduct our travellers as far as the Mond See, eighteen miles distant, the remuneration being fixed at two florins.* Accordingly, on the morning of the 5th, after a good breakfast, they bade adieu to Mr. Jung and started. The road to Thalgau, twelve miles, is pretty and picturesque, over undulating ground, with no very steep ascents, and no very remarkable scenery. It is here a corn-growing country, and the peasants were engaged in gathering in the harvest. It was a day admirably adapted for that purpose, being bright and sunny, rather hot indeed for pedestrians, but not the less enjoyable. Thalgau was reached about one o'clock, and at a clean little *auberge*

THE GUIDE.

in this pretty village, luncheon, consisting of an omelette, the national dish of the poorer Austrians, and in making which they are unsurpassed, was ordered. Whilst this was being prepared, the guide made his appearance and protested his inability to walk further. His shoes, he said, had pinched him, and his feet were so blistered that he could not go on. A council of war was at once held, consisting of the two travellers and the obliging hostess. The resignation of the guide was of course accepted, and his claims were audited by the hostess, who took upon herself the appointment of

---

* An Austrian florin, at the present rate of exchange, is about the value of two francs.

his successor. This having been satisfactorily arranged, justice was done to the excellent luncheon, and the route resumed under the direction of the new guide, at about two o'clock.

The six miles from Thalgau to the Mond See took the travellers over a very lovely country, beautifully wooded, the glorious mountains ever nearer and nearer. As the lake was approached, without however being yet visible, these beauties increased; the tints of the foliage being lovely in their endless variety. At last they came upon the lake itself, nine miles long, with bright clear water, shut in on one side by precipitous rocks, in contrast to which are the prettily wooded banks on the other. Our travellers put up at a little inn called the Krone, situated at the head of the lake, and commanding in the distance a full view of the Schafberg, the giant of the Salzkammergut. The Krone was a decent little inn, very clean and comfortable and kept by an obliging landlady. The water of the lake had however greater attractions for our travellers, who, after a little rest, sallied forth intent to try its depth. After walking along its banks for about ten minutes they suddenly came upon a bathing establishment, consisting of a building with dressing-rooms built out into the lake in deep water for the convenience of swimmers, who were thus able to swim back to their room and dress in comfort. There was an upper story to these rooms where hot coffee was always ready, and which was used as a lounge. This place was the property of one Peter Taffner, a great character, and who also kept a small inn, more popular evidently than the Krone, for it was quite crowded. It appears that the Mond See is a great resort for the holiday-makers of Salzburg and the neighbourhood. The loveliness of the scenery, the pretty walks in the neighbourhood, and the quiet, combine with the excellent arrangements of Taffner to recommend it to those who are in want of rest or recreation. Taffner himself is the model of an obliging host. He is ever cheerful, ever active, ever intent on carrying out the wishes of others. Nor are his charges unreasonable. He informed one of our friends that his terms for board and lodging, including the use of the swimming-rooms and boats, were two florins a day, and that he would take two people for three florins. His little inn seemed clean and comfortable, and, certainly, in so far as the attention of the landlord could conduce to comfort, it would have been impossible to be better off anywhere.

That evening and early the next morning our travellers enjoyed the deep limpid waters of the Mond See. After the second operation they returned to the Krone, and settling with the landlady, started off in a boat, intending to traverse three-fourths of the length of the lake to a little village called Schärfling, whence they would ascend the Schafberg. This mountain, though only about 5,800 feet above the level of the sea, is a great favourite with the Austrians. The ascent is steep, with scarcely a single level or gradual incline to break it. But once on the summit it commands a view, which, in beauty and extent, is not inferior to that enjoyed from the summit of the Rigi. Thence may be seen all the mountains and lakes of the Salzkammergut and Upper Austria, as far as the forests of Bohemia, on the one side; on the other, the snow-clad Alps of Styria, the glorious

Watzmann and Hohe **Göll**, and even, sometimes, the snowy summit of the gigantic **Gross Glockner**. The numberless lakes to be seen in every direction add greatly to the beauty of the panorama, and give to the foreground a life and reality which would otherwise be wanting. The number of lakes visible on a clear day surpasses even the number of those to be seen from the Rigi. On the summit is a little inn, just finished at the time of which we are writing, containing eight bed-rooms and a large *salle-à-manger*. To secure the possession of one of those bed-rooms, it was necessary to be armed with a ticket obtainable only at St. Wolfgang, a village on the high road on the side of the mountain opposite to that on which our travellers were to attempt it. They, therefore, were compelled to trust, in this respect, to chance.

The two friends had a pull of about an hour and a half in the lake before they reached Schärfling. Taking a hasty meal at the little hostelry of that place, and depositing the bulk of their traps with the kind landlady, they started off without a guide,—for the road was not difficult to find,— to make the ascent. A walk of thirty-five minutes took them to the village of Hüttenstein. After passing this, the road makes a turn to the left, and the ascent fairly begins. It is steep, and, as we said, the steepness is continuous. Nevertheless it commands lovely views in every direction, long before the summit is reached, and it was inspiriting to know that the view from that point was the finest of all. In three hours and a half, after a very leisurely walk, that point was reached. No other travellers had arrived. As our friends gained the summit and entered the little inn they were met by a smiling waiter, rubbing his hands, and professing great anxiety to please. He

THE SMILING WAITER.

at once gave them a room on condition that they were to evacuate it in case any ticket-bearing travellers should arrive; even in that event he promised them each a mattress in the *salle-à-manger*. It soon became apparent that it would be necessary to have recourse to this expedient, for travellers came pouring in in great numbers, till not only were the rooms occupied, but it seemed probable that it would be difficult for the *salle*, large as it was, to accommodate all. The new travellers, as they came up, were, however, all met by the same smiling waiter, in the same smiling manner, and all were equally assured of "a mattress at all events,"—the waiter, as he said this, throwing an impressiveness into his manner which it was quite delightful to witness. Our friends, indeed, as they sat waiting for their dinner, could not refrain from taking a great interest in his generalship, and in wondering how he would manœuvre so as not "to break the word of promise to the hope." The *salle* was provided with separate tables, large and small, according to the Austrian fashion, and at these each person dined with his own party. At last all the travellers seemed to have arrived, dinner was served to them in the order in which they had come up, none but the smiling waiter being in attendance. It was wonderful to watch how well he understood his work, how cleverly he waited upon several tables at the same time, never making a mistake. By 9 o'clock his task was apparently over, all the dinners had been eaten, coffee had been served, cigars had been lighted, and all began to think of their mattresses. Our friends, anxious to admit some little fresh air into a room in which so many had dined and were smoking, and upon whose floor some twenty would have to sleep, had even contrived to open, unseen by the multitude, a window in their vicinity. Suddenly, however, just after the waiter had announced his intention of bringing in the mattresses, the door opened, and a cantankerous-looking man, accompanied by three sons, one about eighteen, the other two about fifteen and twelve respectively, entered the room. The man, who was very hot, stood at once in the centre, wiping his face with his handkerchief, and took a good survey about him. All at once his eye fell upon the open window. He immediately preferred a request that it might be shut. This was of course done. He then sat down with his party at the table, and, on the waiter appearing, ordered some wine, saying he could not eat. A pint bottle of light wine having been brought, he proceeded to divide half of it in exact mathematical proportions, according to their size if not according to their age, amongst the three sons, each receiving from about one to three table-spoonsful. The division made did not, however, appear very agreeable to the second son, for, in a most unmistakable manner, he asked for more. This demand having been refused, a controversy ensued between father and son, and continued for about twenty minutes, to the great amusement of the other strangers present, who, having nothing else to do, could only look on. The boy all this time continued deaf to his father's arguments and to insist upon his rights, whereupon the father, to settle the matter, divided the remainder of the wine between himself and the two other boys, to the absolute exclusion of the second, who thereupon abandoned himself to tears. It was past ten o'clock before this matter was settled, and then all began fondly to hope that the mattresses might be brought in. But just as the smiling waiter had arrived apparently at the same conclusion, he was summoned by the cantankerous man and ordered to bring dinner. There was no help for the outsiders, and indeed to Musafir and his friend it was no deprivation, for they derived intense amusement from watching the manners of their neighbours,—all intent on enjoyment; they took advantage, moreover, of the cantankerous man being engaged in his cutlets to re-open the window, and thus to give some relief to the atmosphere of the room. Meanwhile the waiter began to bring in the mattresses. The first of these, which had been placed in a corner, was instantly appropriated by a man with a comical face, a flowing robe and a high-crowned cap, which caused him to bear a striking resemblance to a high priest. This manœuvre of his excited the admiration of his friends, who proceeded to follow his example, amid the general good humour of all. At last all the mattresses had been brought in, twenty-two in number, the cantankerous man finished his coffee, and all prepared to turn in. It was thought, after a short interval, that everyone had turned in, and one of the Austrians was preparing to put out the light, when the voice of the eldest son of the cantankerous man was heard begging him to delay that operation, as his father had gone into the kitchen to dry his clothes. He did not come back for half an hour, and his first act when he did return was to reclose the window, the opening of which had till then happily remained undiscovered. He then proceeded to undress, and arraying himself in an improvised night-cap, which gave him a most fantastic appearance, at length put out the light. The atmosphere of the room was, however, stifling. Upwards of thirty people had dined and smoked in it; now twenty-two were to sleep in it, and all the doors and windows were firmly closed. It appeared to both Musafir and Mercator that such a state of things was scarcely to be borne. Yet as it was impossible to go boldly against public opinion, which had apparently endorsed the act of the cantankerous man, it was determined to effect by subtlety that which could in no other manner be accomplished. Waiting then till all were apparently asleep, Musafir crawled up to one of the windows, and tried to open it; but it was stuck too fast. With a second one he was more successful, and for ten minutes he and his friend revelled in the enjoyment of pure oxygen. But only for ten minutes. At the expiration of that time the voice of the cantankerous man was again heard, begging that the window might be shut. Thenceforth there was no help for it, but in sleep!

At four o'clock everyone rose to watch the effect of the sunrise on the panorama of the distant mountains. A glorious wash in the cold water outside the house somewhat compensated our two friends for the atmosphere inside the room, and they ascended the little elevation above the inn with calmer minds and refreshed bodies. Soon the glorious red disk appeared, illuminating the horizon, tinting the distant snow with his rosy colour, showing a long succession, first of the far-off mountains, then of the varied-coloured hills nearer, then of the clear bright lakes underneath them. To distant Bohemia, to hill-bound Bavaria, to the waters of the Danube on the one side, and to the glaciers of the Gross Glockner on the other, the eye penetrated. Long did they gaze at this glorious picture of nature,—far more splendid, infinitely more glorious and more seductive, than the artificial panoramas which, with the glare of gas-lamps, evoke the astonishment and admiration of the untravelled denizens of towns!

An hour later the two travellers started to descend, doing the journey to Schärfling at a great pace. Under the trees of the garden attached to the little hostelry of that place they had a capital breakfast, then, repossessing themselves of their traps, they entered a narrow canoe-shaped boat and paddled to See-Au, at the extreme end of the lake, the furthest point from that whence they had set out the preceding day. At See-Au they landed, and, shouldering their traps, walked about two miles to Unter-Ach, a little village on the Atter See, the largest lake in the northern part of the Salzkammergut,—it being upwards of fifteen miles in length. On the banks of the lake at Unter-Ach is a clean and comfortable inn, with a sort of pavilion built out into the water, commanding a most lovely view. The beer at Unter-Ach is especially to be commended. The scenery at the lower end of the lake is very pretty indeed, being well wooded and hilly, but the upper part is somewhat bare. A lovely river runs out of it into the Mond See. Our travellers

stayed here only long enough to make arrangements for a
boat to take them to Steinbach, whence it was their inten-
tion to walk across the mountains to the two little gems, the
lakes of Langbath, visited by Musafir and his wife the
previous year. The boat was soon ready, but it required
an hour's hard pulling to reach Steinbach, a rather strag-
gling village on the opposite bank of the lake, and much
higher up it. As there was no road thence to Langbath,
but only a mountain path, amongst many others leading
elsewhere, it was absolutely necessary to engage a guide to
show the way. This was, strange to say, a work of some
difficulty. It was a fête day, and the villagers were enjoying
themselves at the lake and apparently did not much care to
go so far out of their way. However, the offer of two florins
and a half with a meal at the end of it induced a young
fellow to volunteer for the service, and off they started. The
distance to the little inn near the first lake was but twelve
or thirteen miles, but it was the most trying walk our
travellers attempted during their tour. It took them over
a succession of high mountain ridges, very beautiful and
picturesque, but steep and tiring. No sooner had one height
been reached, and the travellers had looked eagerly forward
in the hope of catching a view of the beautiful lake, than
another ascent appeared before them. The pace, too, at
which they had descended the Schafberg told upon them,
and when they reached the little inn at half-past eight in
the evening, they both felt dead beat. It was refreshing
under such circumstances to receive the warm greeting of
the worthy old couple who kept the inn. "It's the Herr
Major," called out the Krähmeyer as they approached,

holding out both his hands to welcome his visitors. Instantly there appeared, in his wake, the old lady with her honest kind face betokening the warmest interest. She was followed by the two servant-girls, smiling their welcome. Questions were asked of all that had happened in the interval, mingled with expressions of pleasure at the renewal of the acquaintance. It transpired in the course of conversation that the little inn was full. The worthy couple, however, insisted upon putting Musafir and his friend into their own room, saying they could easily manage elsewhere for the night. Meanwhile the hostess gave orders for the preparation of a repast in her best style, of which the speckled trout was to form a necessary portion. This was done ample justice to, and the rest of the evening was spent in pleasantly chatting with these honest, warm-hearted Austrians.

Early in the morning, after a plunge in the glorious little basin formed by the river just below the inn, our two friends started to spend the forenoon at the two lakes, the peculiar beauties of which we have already described.* We will only refer to them now to remark that notwithstanding the glowing language in which Musafir had painted them to his companion, Mercator found the reality, especially with respect to the second lake, far surpass the conceptions he had formed. As to Musafir, he thought it then, and he thinks it still, one of the wonders of Europe. Had it been situated in Switzerland it would long before this have been thronged by crowds of tourists; in the course of a few years its simple beauty would have been spoilt by

---

* Pages 32–4.

the erection of artificial grottoes, and vulgar refreshment-rooms; but being in unsophisticated Austria, off the line of rail, and not on the high road, unmarked, or scarcely marked, by the English guide-books, it has happily hitherto escaped defilement of that sort, and still constitutes, in its simple majesty, a place in which nature reigns supreme and triumphant!

That same afternoon our two friends bade farewell to their kind hosts, after many promises—alas! not yet fulfilled* of a future visit, and started in an einspänner for the little village of Traunkirchen on the Gmunden lake. An einspänner is one of the best sort of carriages for mountain travelling. It is a four-wheeled chaise, with a hood, a low seat in front, and a place behind for the luggage. In the seat over which is the hood it can accommodate two people, whilst in front there is a place for the driver, and, if need be, for a fourth person beside him. It is fitted up with arrangements for keeping out rain, and is, altogether, a most comfortable sort of conveyance. In one of these our two travellers drove to Traunkirchen, a distance of only seven miles, and, arriving there, put up at the comfortable little inn facing the giant Traunstein, a rocky mountain rising straight up from the surface of the water to a height of nearly 5,500 feet, and giving by its presence an air of stately grandeur to that part of the lake, in marked and striking contrast to the smiling verdure and green foregrounds, studded with villas, on the other side. The landlord of this little inn did not at all impress

---

* Fulfilled, as we have seen, in 1871.—*Vide* page 87.

our travellers at first sight. He was short and stout, with a swarthy complexion and gloomy air, giving one the idea of a man to whom a smile was unknown, and in whose eyes a hearty laugh was the surest indication of moral turpitude. But a few hours' acquaintance with him was sufficient to dissipate these illusions.

It soon appeared that he was a very good little fellow, rather matter-of-fact indeed, but quite a character in his way. After our friends had finished dinner they invited him, according to the homely Austrian custom, to come and sit at their table, and partake of some wine. It soon appeared that not even an innkeeper is proof against the liquid that "maketh glad the heart of man," for in a few minutes he was engaged in unfolding the principal events of his life. The most important of these had reference to his service in the Austrian army during a period of six years, in the course of which had been fought the battles of Magenta and Solferino, at both of which he "assisted." He was then a corporal, and he complained bitterly—he felt it, he said, even then—of having been kept for three days and three nights without food of any kind. In relating this sad event, his face assumed an expression of agony, which, contrasted with his well-rounded form, was, to our travellers, inexpressibly comic. "But," suggested Mercator, mildly, "it does not appear to have made you thin." "Thin!" shrieked the landlord, with an awful grimace, "I was as thin as a lath, you could have pulled me through a ring; I was just like that"—saying this, he drew in his face hideously. It was evident that he still felt the pangs of those terrible three days. He talked freely of the Austrian generals, and of all but Benedek disparagingly. But his greatest fury was reserved for the mention of the name of Giulay. "The scoundrel," he said, "*hole ihn der Teufel*,—and he draws full-pay to this day!" Many anecdotes of his military life did he relate, almost all personal to himself, with an air of gravity, which, considering that the ludicrous predominated in the stories, was most comical.

We pass over the walk to the Traunfalls, the visit to Gmunden, the drive to Ischl, interesting as they were, because we have already described the impressions made by these places on the mind of Musafir. On reaching Ischl the travellers drove to the Kaiserin Elisabeth, but, it was the height of the season, and that hotel, large as it was, was crowded to the topmost garret. But this did not much signify. The obliging landlord, Herr Endmoser, recommended them to an adjoining hotel, and engaged to procure for them, for next morning, the best guide in the country to conduct them over the mountains to the Grundl See.

Very early next morning they started,—not indeed by the carriage road followed by Musafir and his wife the previous year,—but *viâ* Rettenbach over the Rettenbach Alp, about 5,000 feet high,—one of the most charming walks possible to conceive. There was but a pathway, but it led to most lovely places; some of the gorges being magnificent. The ascent of the Rettenbach was steep, but, once surmounted, the travellers came upon a large plateau of lovely green turf, covered with wild strawberries, at first level, but afterwards descending with an increasing slope towards Alt-Aussee. From this summit were visible, apparently quite close, the shining Dachstein with his field of snow, the stern stony

Loser, causing the Dachstein to shine still more brightly from the contrast, below, and between them and the travellers a smiling green foreground. Not long was this view vouchsafed them. The clouds, then rising from the horizon, soon overspread the heavens, and scarcely had Alt-Aussee been reached, four hours and a half after leaving Ischl, than the rain poured down in torrents. The summer-house, jutting out into the lake, of the little inn at Alt-Aussee was, however, admirably adapted to lunch in on a wet day, and the travellers fondly hoped that before that meal had been consumed, the rain would hold up, and the walk across the hills to the Grundl See be resumed. As, however, the rain still continued to pour, it became necessary to give up the walk across the hills and to proceed to the Grundl See by the road, through Aussee. An hour and a half took our friends to the lake. There, as at Langbath, the greetings were warm and friendly. The hostess was, as usual, demonstrative, but many changes had occurred in the household. Elise, the under-cook, had been allowed to accept the situation of head-cook in a neighbouring inn; whilst Fanny, the Kellnerin, had left to live with her mother, who was infirm. The old Kanzler, however, was there, as anxious as ever to go about with the "Herrschaft." The lake itself, notwithstanding the clouded state of the sky, was as glorious as ever, still soft, beautiful, and bewitching, well deserving the title of the Pride of Styria. Other lakes may indeed surpass this in some one particular point, but in the combination of beauties of all sorts the Grundl See remains unrivalled. It is enchanting in all weathers, and though the day on which our travellers arrived was peculiarly unfavourable, Mercator, who saw it for the first time, was struck with its wonderful loveliness, as well as with the magic effect produced by the quickly passing clouds on the mountains, differing so widely from one another, by which it was surrounded.

At six o'clock next morning—the rain having ceased though the clouds were still hanging about—our travellers walked to the inn, about one-third of the way down the lake, at which Elise was cook, and after partaking of a breakfast prepared by her, were picked up by the Kanzler in a boat, and piloted to the end of the lake. Thence they proceeded to the Töplitz and Kammer Sees. Notwithstanding the weather, the lakes looked most glorious, and it was with regret that the two friends found it impossible to stay there another day. Had they been sure of fine weather it might have been attempted, but the prophets continued to prophesy rain. It began to pour indeed on their return to the inn, and continued so with few intermissions the entire afternoon. Nevertheless, after an early dinner, they tore themselves away and walked twelve miles to Obertraun, a little village on the lake of Hallstadt, the Kanzler leading the way. In fine weather this is a glorious walk; even under the actual circumstances it was enjoyable; for though the rain came down in heavy showers, and the clouds rested on the tops of the mountains, there were occasional breaks, affording lovely peeps, and occasionally disclosing very grand scenery. From Obertraun a boat conveyed them to the little inn, the Grüner Baum, at Hallstadt.

We will not accompany our travellers from Hallstadt to Golling, they having followed the same route as that pursued by the Musafirs the previous year, but this time under the disadvantage of heavy rain, all the low mountains even being covered with snow to within a few hundred feet of the road. At Golling, however, it promised better things, and our travellers determined, therefore, after seeing the waterfall, to cross the Rossfeld Alp, about 5,000 feet high, instead of going round as the Musafirs had done, by Hallein. The other, and loftier, mountain route, that over the Königsberg, was reported by the guides to be impracticable on account of fresh snow having obliterated the pathway. The Rossfeld Alp was accordingly tried. It was a tough walk, some of the ascents being very steep,—but the views from the top were magnificent. Here the travellers were walking, as it were, under the lee of the Hohe Göll, upwards of 8,000 feet high, covered with snow, and producing on its peaks that chaste mountain-flower known as the "edelweiss." The Untersberg too, on the other side of the valley, looked grand with his cap of snow. The effect produced by the appearance, ever and anon, of the sun, shining brilliantly, and driving away the clouds from the snow, was most enchanting. On the top of the Alp, near the boundary between Austria and Bavaria, our travellers came upon an Almhütte, clean and tempting, the shelves of its rooms laden with milk-pans, and the whole presided over by a blue-eyed, fair-haired maiden, as kind and courteous as she was pretty. Our travellers rested here to partake of a bowl of milk, then, pushing on, reached Berchtesgaden six hours after having left Golling. We ought to have stated that the view of this town, during the descent from the Alp, is strikingly picturesque, situated as it is in a lovely undulating valley,

ALI-AFSNE AND THE TRUSSAWASE.

a clear trout-stream running underneath it, and the Watzmann and Untersberg displaying their glories on the background.

Two days were spent in this neighbourhood in inspecting the beauties of the König's See, which we have described in a preceding page. During the whole of this time the weather was very unfavourable, the clouds hanging very low, and the rain coming down with but little intermission. The wondrous beauties of the König's See defy, however, the inclemencies of the weather. Indeed, it is questionable whether the succession of light clouds passing over the mountains, with an occasional peep of sunshine, does not produce a grander effect than the monotony of a clear blue sky, lovely as that is.

In the afternoon the rain came down in torrents, and the weather seemed so unsettled that it was seriously debated whether it would not be more advisable to drive to Salzburg, and take thence the rail to Innsbruck, rather than proceed to Wildbad-Gastein and thence over the mountains to Windisch-Matrey and the capital of Tirol. The two travellers left Berchtesgaden in an *einspänner* before this knotty point had been settled. As they approached the turn of the road leading to Hallein it became necessary to make a decision. In vain was it to look towards the sky. Naught in that direction was visible but a mass of vapour, which, as it neared the earth, seemed to melt into rain. The driver, when appealed to for his opinion, declared it would go on raining for a month. Most dismal seemed the prospects. At length the turn was reached and the driver asked for orders. Without consulting one another both travellers arrived at that moment at one and the same conclusion. They resolved to take the chances of the weather and to hope for better times. The order was accordingly given for Hallein.

The first thing on arriving there was to take places in the mail-coach for Wildbad Gastein. The stage-coaches on the high roads in Austria are most comfortable conveyances, quite as much so as a private carriage. There is, moreover, this advantage connected with them; that, if a traveller take a place in the coach over-night, and the coach, on arrival, happen to be full, the postmaster is bound to furnish a separate carriage for the individual. On this occasion there was plenty of room available, and our travellers started early on the following morning. They drove through Golling, Pass Lueg—one of the grandest and most magnificent passes in Europe, and which a few hundred men could hold against an army,—through Werfen, Lend—after leaving which is a magnificent gorge,—Dorf Gastein, and Hof Gastein, arriving at the late hour of nine at Wildbad Gastein. There they put up at the Hirsch, there being no room at the crack hotel, Straubinger's.

Gastein is a lovely place, situated in a basin from all sides of which rise the lofty green mountains. It abounds in cataracts and waterfalls, and from it the most enjoyable excursions may be made. Of these the principal are Böckstein, three, and Nassfeld, seven, miles distant. From this a splendid view is to be obtained of the giant of the Noric Alps, the Gross Glockner, 12,369 feet above the sea, and its lovely glaciers. In fact at Nassfeld the traveller stands, as it were, within the precincts of that noble mountain. The still falling rain took away from our travellers the hope they had previously entertained of crossing the glaciers to Heiligenblut, but in the afternoon the clouds dispersed and the sun appeared in all his glory. It seemed even possible that the journey might be attempted, and an application was accordingly made to the guide who possessed the greatest reputation in the place, and who rejoiced in the name of Haas. This man, however, declared that the attempt to cross the pass after the fresh snow that had fallen would be most dangerous, that the tracks had all been obliterated, and that he would not make the venture for the world. On leaving him, somewhat crestfallen, our travellers met another guide, named Freyberger. This man gave an opinion exactly contrary to that of Haas. He declared that there was no difficulty in the trip, and that the fallen snow made it only the easier. The German guide-books, which were available, appeared rather to strengthen the opinion offered by Haas; nevertheless, Freyberger seemed so confident, he was so ready to risk himself, and our travellers were so anxious to go, that they were most unwilling to give him up lightly. In this extremity they determined to ask the opinion of the oldest inhabitant of the place, Mr. Straubinger, the owner of Straubinger's hotel, and whose family has flourished in Gastein for three centuries, as to the relative merits of the two guides. If Mr. Straubinger should state that Freyberger was as much to be depended upon as Haas, then it was determined to follow him and start on the expedition.

Though our travellers were not staying in his hotel,

Mr. Straubinger met them with truly Austrian courtesy, listened patiently to their question regarding the merits of the two guides, and then said very decidedly that Haas was the better man of the two, and, in all matters referring to the mountains, was the more implicitly to be relied upon. He then, in reply to a question, stated that, in such weather, he considered the proposed trip one of very doubtful safety. It would have been hazardous to act against such an opinion; most reluctantly, therefore, the expedition was given up.

Perhaps, at the time, there was no alternative; for our travellers were personally unacquainted with the mountain, and the weight of evidence was against them. Nevertheless, they both regretted their decision, and they had afterwards collateral evidence that the attempt might have been safely made. Haas, it appeared, had almost given up the duties of a guide, and had taken to trading, whilst Freyberger lived by excursions such as these.

The resolve, however, having been taken, they returned next day to Lend, determined to proceed thence, along the valley of the Pinzgau, to Innsbruck. This valley as far as Mittersill is the most uninteresting valley in Tyrol, being low, marshy, and commanding no good view, notwithstanding that from many points in it most lovely excursions may be made. Our travellers, too, made a great mistake, in that, on arriving at Mittersill, they did not take the lower road to Krimml, Gerlos, and Zell in Zillerthal, but followed the upper and far less interesting route to Kitzbühel. Both led equally to Innsbruck, but it was a pity to miss the splendid gorges and magnificent cataract of

Krimml, finer than any in Switzerland, the snowy valleys of Gerlos, and the domestic gaiety of the inhabitants of Zell. The fact was that the travellers had fully counted on being able to cross to the southern side of the Alps, and had neglected to study the route on the northern side. It was a great mistake, but it at all events marked Krimml and its neighbourhood as places to be visited on the earliest opportunity.

We pass over this uninteresting valley, and take our travellers to Innsbruck. How is it possible to describe this wonderful city, with the mountains, 9,000 feet high, so overhanging the town, that, it is said, the wolves peep over the summit to see what is passing in the streets;—the golden-roofed house,—the wonderful churches,—that one especially which contains the statues of imperial and royal personages, among them that of Arthur, King of England,—and its many interesting associations? From Schloss Ambrass, a castle, about two miles away from the town, the view of it is magnificent, picturesque and striking beyond description. Perhaps indeed the town itself does not look altogether so imposing as Salzburg from the Capuzinerberg, but it is not in itself less interesting, for here the place is peopled in imagination by the sturdy sons of liberty who knew how to die rather than submit to the yoke of the foreigner. Such a place it is impossible to describe, nor is description necessary. It is a city which must be seen to be appreciated, which deserves to be visited over and over again. On each occasion of his return the traveller will be more and more struck with the natural wonders which make Innsbruck so loveable. We may add that there are capital inns and shops, and that it is always feasible, as it is indeed in every large town in Austria, to change notes, both circular and Austrian, for gold, and *vice versâ*.

The weather became again threatening as the travellers left Innsbruck, proceeding by coach to Landeck, whence it was their intention, in conformity with the original plan, to walk through the Finstermünz Pass, and over the Stelvio, into Italy. From Landeck, a return carriage took them to Ried, whence they walked—nine miles—to Pfunds, the valley becoming more and more picturesque as they went on. At Pfunds they put up at a little inn, called the "Traube," the type of a Tyrolese inn, so clean were the rooms, so kind and attentive the hostess. For their dinner here, including a bottle of Tyrolese wine, their bed-rooms, and their breakfast, the travellers were charged the extremely moderate sum of three shillings and eight-pence. Yet nothing could have been better than their fare!

Next day they were to walk through the famous Finztermünz Pass, nearly 3,300 feet above the level of the sea. It is a gradual ascent from Pfunds, with very grand scenery, second only, indeed, to the *Via Mala*. The Pass was formed by the river Inn, which by forcing its way from the Engadin valley, made this cleft in the mountains. It constitutes now a splendid defensive position, and has been fortified by the Austrians in such a manner as to make it almost impregnable. After leaving the little village of Nauders, beyond Finstermünz, the traveller, if he look back, enjoys a most splendid view of the pass, rising from the narrow cleft, through which the Inn flows rapidly, to a point, the height of which that very narrowness tends, in appearance, to increase. About an hour after leaving Nauders the road rather descends, and half an hour later the village of Reschen is reached. Here the scene is entirely altered. The green foliage of the pass entirely disappears; and the traveller approaches gradually an undulating ground, called the common, or pasture land, of Mals, famous as the spot on which the Swiss finally defeated the Austrians in 1499, and achieved their independence. Beyond this again, soaring far above every other mountain, is the snow-covered Ortler, nearly 13,000 feet above the sea, every peak capped with snow, and shining with glaciers innumerable. This is now the traveller's land-mark, for under the lee of the Ortler he must pass over the Stelvio!

It is difficult to describe, but many of our readers have doubtless experienced, the wonderful beauties that open out to a traveller as he approaches a gigantic snow-mountain; now the haze, caused by distance, imperceptibly clears off, and beauty after beauty is disclosed; now the outline, at first perhaps dim, becomes sharp and vigorous; the snow, from being a vague mass of white, shines more brightly than polished ivory; now, as its base is approached, the height of the mountain seems more and more overwhelming. What magic is there in the crowded theatres or the densely packed ball-rooms equal to this? Every step forward is a delight of the purest character. On that spot have these mountains remained fast since the creation of the world! Here they have welcomed the sun, the rain, and the hail;— on their heads the lightning has darted innocuously his forked javelin; the rise and fall of peoples, of nations, of kingdoms, of generations, have taken place around them, and yet they are unaltered; the mountain which the patriot Swiss invoked in 1499, in their decisive struggle with the mailed cavalry of Austria, is still, nearly four hundred years later, the great object of interest to the peaceful traveller. It remains the very same, whilst all around changes and is changing. Or, if there be any difference, it is this, that these mountains, believed by our forefathers to be sacred from the foot of the stranger, have yielded in this nineteenth century to the energy and perseverance of English mountaineers, and that there is scarcely one of them that does not bear upon its summit the symbol of the undaunted nature of the great Anglian race!

At Mals, which our travellers reached that evening, after a walk of twenty-one miles, there is a diverging of two roads, the one leading by Prad to Trafoi, a small village whence the ascent of the Ortler is generally made, thence over the Stelvio into Italy, the other *viâ* Naturns to Meran, the heart of the Tyrol. The former was the route of our travellers. But, as it was a matter of some importance with them to reach Bormio that evening they drove to Trafoi, breakfasted there at a clean little inn, and then commenced the ascent. The road over the Stelvio was formerly considered one of the wonders of the engineering art; but since the war of 1859, which severed Lombardy from Austria, its repairs have been neglected, and at the time of our travellers' visit it was gradually falling into decay. For pedestrians however it was still, and will ever be, easy to be traversed. From Trafoi to the summit is one of the loveliest walks possible to imagine. Under the lee, as we have said, of the Ortler, every turn discovers some new beauty.

The Ortler itself is quite close to the path traversed, and the snow-flakes were clearly visible. In three hours, the summit, 9,000 feet above the sea, was reached. Here the snow was under them and all about them; the highest point of the Ortler had been left behind; and before them was Italy ! It was an exhilarating feeling. To be thus on the summit of the highest pass in Europe, the air so fresh and bracing, and below, the classic land, rich in a thousand recollections, and whose people had, after years of oppression, roused themselves to a sense of the value of the natural birthright of the human race. For all practical purposes, Italy, at least that mountainous part of it visited by our travellers, is still far behind Austria. It is curious that within the distance of a few miles this difference should be so strongly marked. But so it is. Descending the mountain, our friends reached, in half an hour, the little inn of Santa Maria, where they had resolved to lunch. It became at once perceptible that they were in Italy. A dirty table-cloth instead of the clean linen always offered even in the humblest villages of Austria; greasy cookery; bad attendance; and exorbitant charges; made it clear to them that the frontier had been passed. To Musafir the evidence of the fact was equally brought home in another manner. Hitherto, though Mercator could speak German, Musafir had acted as spokesman, and had managed the trip: alike in Austria, in the Pinzgau, and in Tyrol, he had hailed the opportunity of airing his knowledge of the language. But in crossing the frontier his occupation was gone; he did not then understand a word of Italian; all the arrangements were, therefore, for the two days they were in Italy, confided to Mercator, who possessed a conversational knowledge of that language. They could not indeed have been made over to better hands; but the feeling of helplessness which ignorance of the language of a country always induces came home to Musafir with double force after the pleasantness of his German experiences, and he inwardly registered a vow to make himself acquainted with Italian before again venturing on the soil of Italy. Nothing is more true than that a knowledge of the language of the country quadruples the pleasures of foreign travel.

The descent from Santa Maria to Bormio being uninteresting, and it being somewhat late in the day, our travellers hired an *einspänner* to take them there, Mercator chatting all the time with the driver in a most provoking manner. The mountain scenery was wild, rugged, and solitary. At Bormio, however, the scene changes. Near this place is a large bathing establishment, consisting of a grand hotel with hot-water baths attached to it. These baths are supplied from saline sulphureous springs, the water of which has a green tint. Some of them are large enough to swim in. Such temptations were not to be resisted, and though a doubt may exist as to whether a plunge into a saline sulphureous bath is, in itself, a thing to be relished, there can be none as to its powers of refreshing after a long day's work. This hotel at Bormio is infinitely preferable to the inns in the town, and is a most luxurious establishment. The country around is very pretty.

Our travellers started the next day for Tirano in an *einspänner*. After continuing the descent for some time, they came gradually into a valley, very fertile and well populated, and which realised the preconceived ideas of sunny Italy. It was extremely bright and pretty, the hill-sides being covered with vines, which were cultivated with studious care by the strong-limbed and picturesquely-clad population. Soon was reached the valley of the Adda. The road along the banks of this river was, however, in a perilous condition in consequence of the recent floods, and in one part had entirely been washed away. But by the aid of the peasantry the carriage was taken over the dilapidated spot without much delay. Thence to Tirano the road lay through the same bright sunny scenery. Our travellers passed through that rather deserted-looking town, and went on a quarter of a mile further to Madonna-di-Tirano, a little village at the foot of the pass leading to Puschiavo,—the drive from Bormio having taken four hours and a half. At this village there is a fine church, famous for its wood-carving. The little inn, too, is tolerable, though inferior to those on the Austrian side. In the square in front of it, the Bersaglieri had just turned out for bayonet exercise. Very smart fellows they looked, though by no means equal, in Musafir's opinion, to that splendid body the Chasseurs de Vincennes, or to the Jäger regiments of the Austrians. After luncheon the route was resumed for Puschiavo. This was for five miles a glorious walk up a magnificent gorge. About one mile from Madonna the Swiss frontier was crossed. Soon after it came down to pour in torrents. This rather spoiled the pleasure of the afternoon's excursion, and, indeed, was the cause of considerable inconvenience to Musafir, for having walked to the top of the gorge in the rain, and become completely soaked through, he incautiously seated

himself in his wet clothes in an *einspänner*, and drove for
three miles to Puschiavo, thereby catching a cold so severe
as to take from him the power of walking the next day. It
was indeed a caution to travellers. At the top of the gorge,
the lovely lake of Puschiavo was reached. Here is a grand
hotel with baths, apparently most comfortable. The situa-
tion is beautiful, and the hotel would make capital head-
quarters for a month or two in the summer. The lake is
full of trout, and surrounded by prettily-wooded hills, whilst
the glorious range of the Bernina, with its magnificent
glaciers, towers up a few miles beyond. To be able to start,
so as to cross that range on the morrow, our travellers did
not remain at the lake, but pushed on three miles further to
the town of Puschiavo. Here their Italian driver, who had
imbibed so freely as not to be master of his actions, and who
relieved himself by shouting alternately in favour of Victor
Emanuel and of Garibaldi, took them to a den, which, how-
ever, looked so uninviting, that, as he obstinately refused
to move, they left him, and, shouldering their traps, went
themselves in search of a more decent-looking hostelry.
They soon found one, the hotel Albricci, kept by the most
obliging people, and in cleanliness and comfort vying with
the inns of Austria. The daughter of the house, who seemed
to manage everything, was extremely comely, and had the
most charming manners. She spoke Italian so prettily,
that the drawback of not being able to talk or understand
that language was more than ever deplored. Nothing could
exceed the kindness and attention with which the wants of
our travellers were attended to at this little inn; nor were
such services unduly charged for,—the bill being moderate

in the extreme. The little town is prettily situated, being at the foot, as it were, of the Bernina Pass. It would not, however, be ordinarily much frequented by travellers, as these would probably prefer the hotel on the lake of Puschiavo on the one side, or Pontresina, Samaden, or St. Moritz, on the other.

Next morning our travellers started to cross the Bernina Pass to Samaden. Musafir being quite unable to walk from the cold that had attacked him, it was necessary to charter an *einspänner*. The morning was dull, and the clouds were very low; still hopes were entertained of being able to cross the pass before the rain should actually fall. For two-thirds of the way it held up, though the heavy clouds quite obscured the view. Suddenly, however, just as they were turning a corner, the storm, preceded by a terrible howl, burst upon them. Such a storm as it was! Wind in all its fury, succeeded by heavy rain; the rain in its turn giving way to snow, and the snow again to rain. The carriage was then at a height of about 4,000 feet, on a narrow ledge of a road, with precipices underneath. The wind blew in such gusts that it appeared more than once as though it would blow the little vehicle off its balance. Fortunately, however, a place of refuge was at hand. A little inn, called La Rosa, was within a few hundred feet of the travellers, and this was, though with difficulty, reached. Meanwhile the thunder was pealing all around them, and the forked lightning was beyond description vivid. Though but a short time exposed to the violence of the storm, the hail had collected in masses on the apron of the carriage, and the horse and driver had been most thoroughly drenched. The delight of a little inn, humble as this was, with a cheering fire and warm soup, cannot be described. The cold was even then great. A few minutes later there arrived for the same shelter a lady and gentleman coming from the opposite direction. They described the cold on the top of the pass as being absolutely intense, not to be encountered driving without many more wraps than those which our travellers possessed. There seemed no help for it, however. But when, three hours later, the storm abated and the other travellers went down the hill, the kind landlord lent to our friends a blanket and a great-coat on the promise that they should be returned the next day from Samaden. They then started, the sun coming out immediately afterwards, and disclosing a panorama unrivalled in beauty of that peculiar kind. The air was clear and cold, the sky blue, but all around them was snow. The peaks of the Bernina are particularly striking in their form, and their snowy covering shone brilliantly in the bright sun; there was a wildness about the scene which was most captivating, and it was difficult to resist the fanciful impression that the wolves of the nursery story were hovering in the distance ready to follow the track of the wearied horse. The cold was terrific. Never had either of the travellers felt anything approaching to it. The wraps lent by the host, though intended for winter use, could not keep it out. It pierced to the very bones.

At length the summit was reached. Here are two little lakes, each with a character of its own. One is formed of glacier water, a yellowish brown in colour; the other is bright blue. The contrast of this latter with the white snow was very beautiful. But who shall describe the cold? Here

the full force of the wind, sweeping over the Monte Rosso, or
coming up from the Pontresina valley, was upon them. It
was scarcely to be borne. Still there was no choice but to
go on. At last, three-quarters of an hour after leaving the
height, a little inn, the Osteria Bernina, came in view. A
halt was made; our travellers alighted, though, especially
Musafir, with difficulty. A glass of hot brandy-and-water
soon, however, restored the circulation, and they accom-
plished the remainder of their journey to Samaden without
let or hindrance of any kind,—the air becoming perceptibly
warmer as they proceeded. It was still cold, not so much
so, however, as to prevent the enjoyment of the lovely Alpine
scenery which presented itself to the gaze in this most lovely
valley. First there was the Morteratsch glacier,—the finest
in Switzerland,—most glorious to behold; the Rosegg
glacier, smaller though scarcely less grand; Pontresina, the
head-quarters of Alpine Club men, most prettily situated on
a green spot on the banks of a sparkling, swiftly-flowing river,
—the heights of Monte Oro and Monte Rosso towering
above. These, however, are but the salient points. The
place is sparkling with beauty and brightness. From the
windows of the little inn at Samaden, called the "Bernina
Aussicht," the view is magnificent. There is the green
patch of Pontresina, the clear sparkling river, the wonderful
glaciers and the snowy giants in the background. Of its
kind it is unsurpassed if not unrivalled.

This is the valley which an Anglo-Indian, with sound
lungs and suffering only from the effects of long residence
in India, should resort to. Though called a valley, it is
nearly as high as the top of the Rigi. Its climate is

described by the residents as being " nine months winter, and three months cold." But during those three months cold, the rest of Europe suffers three months of intense heat. The cold in this valley—called the valley of the Engadin—during this period is of the most healthy character. It is dry, bracing, and, to the last degree, invigorating. There is nothing like it anywhere else. Here a man feels that he can breathe; he soon ceases to be an invalid, and he pants then to climb those glorious heights which have yielded, one and all, though after much perseverance, to the daring energy of the members of the Alpine Club.

It is well worthy of remark, too, that in this valley the houses and villages are scrupulously clean, and the people more than ordinarily obliging. So great has been the increase in the number of visitors of late years that each village has several comfortable inns. Those of Samaden, Pontresina, Silva Plana and St. Moritz are perhaps most to be commended, but there are doubtless others. Sure we are that in any of these the invalid Anglo-Indian will speedily recover his faded vitality, and with it that elasticity of spirits which is the natural gift of those mountain regions.

But our tour has almost come to a close. After booking a parcel containing the coat and blanket to the kind host of La Rosa, our travellers, pressed for time, prepared to start by coach for Chur,—the air of the Engadin having driven away Musafir's indisposition. Driving through the pretty village of Silva Plana with its two charming lakes and glorious views of snow, our travellers crossed then the Julier Pass, about 6,800 feet, bare, rugged, and uninteresting, till they reached Mühlen. Thence to Tiefenkasten, a village romantically situated in the bottom of a valley, the view grows gradually prettier; and occasionally some **remarkably fine bits are to be seen.** It is pretty for the remainder of the way. Darkness had however set in before our travellers were landed at the Hotel Luckmanier in Chur.

Once more on the line of rail they proceeded along the valley of the Vorder Rhine to Ragatz. The visit to the famous **Bad** Pfäffers, about three miles from this place, may be regarded as the last, as it was the least considerable, of their pedestrian excursions. To Pfäffers the road runs immediately along the banks of the Tamina, a high and continuous wall of rock rising up from the opposite side of the river. The effect of the dark stream running under this rock is very fine indeed, and the walk is extremely pretty. But it is at the baths themselves that admiration is forced even from those whom long gazing at the marvellous has palled. Imagine a deep gorge with high rocks on either side, now open at the top and showing the green trees and blue sky above, now closed so as to make all dark below; at the bottom of the gorge, several hundred feet below the surface, there dashes fiercely along a dark, turbid stream, at one turn of which the ascending steam proclaims the existence of a hot spring, so hot that the atmosphere in its vicinity resembles that of a vapour bath. By degrees the eye becomes accustomed to the dim light, and, glancing upwards, notices what, perhaps, is the greatest wonder of all. Along the rocks, high up, even near the summit, are long lines of water-marks, showing clearly that some thousands of years ago that dark river ran its course nearly level with the summit. It could have been no sudden fall,—that which the traveller here sees,—it must have been the gradual work of long ages. The sinking of the line was probably unnoticed in any single age; it must have been gradual as the passing of a man's life, imperceptible to mortal eye. It is very wonderful, and very suggestive.

Leaving Ragatz, our travellers proceeded to the Hotel Baur at Zurich, and parted the day after at Basel. Their tour was over. It had been a most delightful one,—a little cramped, perhaps, by the shortness of the period allotted for it, but in every other respect most enjoyable. On counting up expenses it was found that this tour of nearly a month's duration, in which economy had by no means been studied, had not cost each more than fifteen pounds! With so small a sum is so much enjoyment to be realised in Europe!

We now proceed to indicate, as briefly as may be, the amount of wardrobe, and the other requisites, to which it may be possible for a tourist to confine himself. The wants of a man are few. The inns on the road provide everything except wearing apparel and soap. At these, too, he can always arrange to have his linen and under-garments washed. Giving these out at four or five in the afternoon, he can always have them in the morning. He will be amply supplied, therefore, if, of under-garments, he have three of each sort. For pedestrian excursions no shirts are to be compared to those made of silk; they fold into a small compass, and even when wet through they keep out the cold to a far greater extent than flannel. Of outer clothing the traveller should take one suit, consisting of a coat, waistcoat, and knickerbockers. These last are far preferable to trousers, especially in wet weather, and, if the traveller be

a fisherman, it is always easy to keep the **knickerbockers dry,
and at the most a change of stockings is involved.** The
best material is a smooth-surfaced tweed, and the best **colour
a grey.** A coat made **of** Russian **duck may be likewise
taken, as it may be worn with advantage** when **the heat of
the sun makes the other almost unbearable. We would
recommend** him also to take a light black **coat and waistcoat
and** a pair of **trousers. It is** not respectful **to the inhabi-
tants of a large** city **to** appear **at the** *table d'hôte* **of** its
principal hotel in the costume of a vagrant. Such a costume
should be reserved **for** the **mountains. In a town** the
ordinary dress of towns-people should **be** worn. **It is**
astonishing how **the** fair fame **of our** countrymen **has**
suffered **by** a neglect of this simple custom. **A light shower-
proof overcoat is quite as serviceable as a mackintosh and
infinitely more comfortable. These are** obtainable **all over
the** Continent. In Germany **they are** called **" wetter
mantel,"** and cost but a few shillings. **These are as service-
able, though, perhaps, not so elegant, as those** purchased in
England at **a** higher price. **No hat is so comfortable or so
serviceable as** the soft high-crowned felt **hat of** the **Austrian**
mountaineers ; **it is far** pleasanter **to wear than any English-
made hat, it keeps out** the **rain, and** its broad brim wards off
the sun from the **face. They** have this additional **advantage
that in Austria everyone wears them. Of shoes we would**
recommend that two pairs **should be taken, both to lace up
in front, but one pair rather** thicker **than the other. It is
easy to have them** " nailed " **in any part of Austria. A good**
umbrella **is indispensable as a protection against the sun,
more even than** against **the rain. It should be attached to**

a good stout stick pointed with iron, so as to be used, if needful, in climbing. An Alpine stock is only necessary in the higher ranges. For a bag to carry these things not one is equal to the Austrian *rücksack*, which may be obtained for a few shillings in any town or village.

Admirable maps may be procured anywhere. For Austria, the Tyrol, and Bavaria, those by Mayr are the best; for Carinthia and Carniola those by Justus Perthes, of Gotha, cannot be surpassed; for Switzerland there are several, but probably that prepared under the auspices of the Alpine Club, published by Messrs. Longman & Co., is by a long way the best. The most useful guide-book for the whole of Germany is Baedeker's. It is not to be surpassed, and his recommendations for the hotels can always be relied upon. His Swiss guide-book is equally good, but he has a rival in M. Berlepsch, a Swiss, and a practical mountaineer. It is only fair to say that both are excellent.

To provide for a change of seasons it is always open to the traveller to send on a box of clothes to any town which lies on his route to await his arrival there. Having changed or replenished his stock he can again send it on to another place. This custom is well understood all over the Continent, and is constantly resorted to.

A few days' experience will show the traveller in what respect his stock is deficient. It is always easy to replenish it at any town. It is better in the mountains not to have anything in excess. The addition of one or two pounds to a heavy bag is often sufficient to make a guide refuse to carry it.

We turn now, with diffidence, to the lady's outfit. This is

a very difficult question. Ladies are so accustomed to an excessive wardrobe in India, that they find it difficult to believe that they can ever accustom themselves to one of the diminutive nature requisite for a mountain excursion. Yet we have never known an instance in which a lady, taking with her at the outset "the very least she must have," did not find at the end of a month that she had more than double her actual requirements. The fact is that excess of baggage becomes a nuisance and an encumbrance. It is soon found that with the many conveniences offered by the inns in the shape of washing, a small quantity supplies the wants as well as a large one, whilst it is infinitely more handy. A lady, therefore, whatever may have been her previous ideas on the subject, would always be eager to propose to discard the superfluous. That may be waiting for her at the nearest town. There can be no object in dragging silk dresses across the mountains. Two dresses, indeed, are ample for all purposes of travel, the one condition being that both shall be of strong material. Stout boots lined with flannel, a shower-proof cloak reaching almost to the heels, a useful hat,—none can be more so than that of the Styrian form worn by men and very becoming when used by ladies,—a small umbrella, and some good warm wraps. Fortunately it is no longer necessary to talk about crinolines, than which no article of dress is more out of place in the mountains. Changes of garments can always be sent on to await arrival, if necessary, at the first large town on the road.

The expenses of travelling in Austria are not very great. As a rule a party of gentlemen can do it for much less than a mixed party of ladies and gentlemen; but in neither case is it ruinous. The pleasantest number for a party is four, two of whom should be ladies. Four can fill one large carriage or two *einspänners*; four will generally be able to find accommodation even in a rustic inn; and in that magic number are companionship and society. The entire expenses of a party of four ought not to exceed from £60 to £80 per mensem, inclusive of everything, or from £15 to £20 a head. Much depends on the length of the halts at each place. The enjoyment of travelling is greatly increased by the knowledge on the traveller's part that there is no limit as to time; that he can stay as long as he pleases at each place; that the season is absolutely at his disposal. There are many places, such for instance as the Grundl-See and the lakes of Langbath, the beauties of which cannot be thoroughly examined under a week or ten days, and which it is difficult to quit even then. In a long trip, with several halts of this sort, the mere expenses of travelling are spread over a longer period, and lessen proportionately the monthly expenditure. There are few Anglo-Indians who could not well afford such an outlay as that we have mentioned. It ought, in Austria and Bavaria, in no case to exceed the larger sum. In Switzerland it would probably be nearly doubled.

It is, however, essential to the comfort, and it will add greatly to the enjoyment, of a party of travellers, that one at least of their number shall understand the language of the country through which they are passing. We think it was Charles V. who said that a man has as many separate existences as he knows languages, and all experience goes

to confirm the truth of the apothegm of the great emperor.
The knowledge of a new language most certainly opens out
to a man a new world. He reads not only the thoughts of
great men as they expressed them in books, but he has
opportunities in conversation for the study of character, and
for acquainting himself with habits and manners, not other-
wise attainable. The attempt, too, to acquire a new language
constitutes a delightful study, alike enlarging the mind and
contributing to strengthen the resources which every man,
it is supposed, possesses, to a greater or lesser degree, in
himself. Few things, moreover, tend more to give a man
self-confidence, and to foster independence of thought and
feeling, than a knowledge of languages. Any knowledge
gained by the independent action of the mind must show
the possession of a certain amount at least of sterling quali-
ties. It must show perseverance, energy, a determination
not to be baffled, a power to withstand temptation to amuse-
ments, when something more important is in view. Above
all, it trains a man to travel on that road which is the
surest path-way to success—the road which leads without
a single deviation to a pre-determined end. Now, success
in study, which is only accomplished by the exercise of those
qualities, immensely strengthens them. It assures the
man of his capacity to succeed in other things. It thus
gives him confidence in himself, and that self-confidence is
the parent of the independence of thought, without which a
man is necessarily a machine.

In India, which, in the present day at all events, is
regarded by few but as a resting-place, the study of European
languages ought, one would think, to be peculiarly attractive.

At the great places of resort on the continent of Europe the tone of society corresponds far more to that of India than does the tone of society in England. At those places people meet for pleasure, acquaintances are easily made, and a very agreeable society is thus formed. There is no occasion here for letters of introduction, or formal presentations. All meet on the same footing, it being generally understood that only those travel who can afford to do so. A visit to the Continent during the summer and autumn would, then, offer strong temptations to those Anglo-Indians who consider English manners and habits peculiarly repelling. Yet, as many of them have found, a journey on the Continent, unaccompanied by a knowledge of the language by one at least of the party, is often rank misery. In fact, to our mind, it is of all social miseries the greatest. It is a repetition of the tortures of Tantalus. The traveller sees how much there is capable of enjoyment, and yet that that enjoyment is withheld from him—by ignorance of the language!

If people in India knew how easy it is to acquire some rudiments, at least, of a continental language, we are sure they would not be diverted from the study by the temptation of those second-rate pleasures which India can alone offer. To our mind India is the place of all others best fitted for the study of the drier portions of a foreign language. We can understand that in Europe, where there is so much to tempt a man into the sunshine and open air, where the streams invite the angler, the slopes of the mountain the botanist, the forests the sportsman, and where the merry laugh and innocent smiles of the daughters of the land invite all,—it must require the virtue of a St. Anthony to persevere regularly in such studies. But in dull, prosy India, in which the men are so care-worn and mysterious, and the society is a society of cliques, in which there are few temptations to ramble out of doors, and where everyone seems bent on maintaining or increasing his social position, a study of that sort is a refuge from a world which, in their hearts, few can find congenial. In a country in which everyone complains of a want of occupation, this is of all occupations the most delightful and the most repaying. It is easily accomplished, even if it is impossible, for the moment, to obtain a master. The system of Ollendorf has been made applicable to all the languages of Europe. A key is attached to each exercise-book. Sooner or later the student is sure to meet with an Italian, a Frenchman, or a German, who will be glad to impart to him the mysteries of the pronunciation. He quickly becomes interested in his task; somewhat later, and all the difficulties of the grammar are surmounted—he is able to read, even to speak a little. He will not then require any incitement to persevere. He is at the portals of a new world, and nothing then can restrain him from culling its fruits.

The desire thus to learn—how many possess it? The perseverance requisite for the task—who will admit that they have it not? It is a great quality, greater even than genius; and it has this peculiarity, that it is capable of being acquired by all who have force of will. It is a quality which gains strength by being used, which increases in intensity as the will becomes more firm, the aim more direct. We may be sure of this, that without such a quality nothing great can be accomplished : unsupported by it, a man will be more and more inclined to grovel in the narrow lanes of life : great thoughts, noble instincts, will gradually desert him. Possessing it, there is scarcely any aim so high, to which a man otherwise capable, may not aspire.

We conclude, then, our last account of Musafir's wanderings by expressing a hope that a perusal of it may induce others, ladies as well as gentlemen, to qualify themselves for the perfect enjoyment of that pleasure, which, of all those offered to Anglo-Indians on their return to Europe, is the simplest, the most health-giving, the most delightful.

THE END.

www.ingramcontent.com/pod-product-compliance
Lightning Source LLC
Chambersburg PA
CBHW031443160426
43195CB00010BB/831